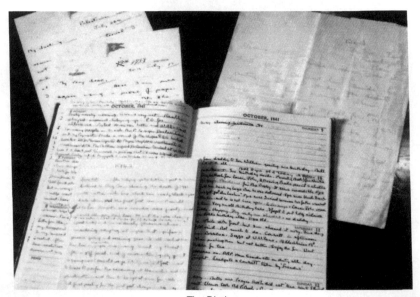

The Diaries.

Mrs. Elsie Crouch

Her Diaries 1941–1942

Mrs. Elsie Crouch
Her Diaries 1941–1942

Editor
Bill Crouch

ASPECT DESIGN

Mrs Elsie Crouch: Her Diaries 1941–1942
Compiled and Edited by Bill Crouch

Designed and Printed by Aspect Design 2010
Malvern, Worcestershire, United Kingdom.
Designed and Printed by Aspect Design
89 Newtown Road, Malvern, Worcs. WR14 1PD
United Kingdom
Tel: 01684 561567
E-mail: books@aspect-design.net
Website: www.aspect-design.net

ISBN 978-1-905795-62-8

CONTENTS

LIST OF ILLUSTRATIONS

Photographs are listed clockwise from top left of each page

INTRODUCTION

The Diaries, one in a small, rather ragged notebook and the other just a few pages without a cover, were in a pile of photographs and other odds and ends which, my sister, Eleanor took charge of after our mother died in 1969. They must have lain unattended for years until at a family get-together, I expressed my interest in doing our family history and they surfaced again. Even so, it was another few years before I really looked into this box and discovered just what a treasure we had. The writing was difficult to read, some of it was in pencil, and so I decided to transcribe them for the family.

When they were written, I was 5 years old and Eleanor 3. The war had been going for some 2 years and, as you will see, times were very tough. Our father, Will, was a Warrant Officer (Regimental Sergeant Major) in Malta serving with the Royal Corps of Signals. He was posted there in April, 1936, and Mum joined him after I was born in October 1936 in Leadgate, Co

Durham. Eleanor was born in the Military Families Hospital, Imtarfa in Malta in May 1938. In July 1939, with war looming, Mum, Eleanor and I returned to UK along with many other army families, in the 'Palestinian Prince'. We went to live with Mum's sister Ella Jewitt and their mother, Isabella Jewitt, a widow. And there the family remained. Dad was in Malta throughout the terrible siege there and returned to us in 1943.

Mum's father had been a miner in the Leadgate pit and he died in August 1938. This must have hit Mum hard. She had another sister, Eve, who was the eldest and a brother, George who was the youngest. Eve lived in Delves Lane just outside Consett and was a constant visitor with her son, John. Her husband, Ralph Nolloth, worked at Consett Ironworks, a reserved occupation. George was married to Queen and lived in Dunchurch near Rugby.

Dad's family lived in Bournemouth. His mother, Dora, was also a widow; her husband had died in 1923. Dad was the eldest child and he had two brothers. Cyril was in the RAF and Ron in the Royal Artillery. Ron's wife Elsye was living with Nan until, as Mum writes in 1942, Elsye moved out and Joan went to live with her instead.

Ella went off to do war work in a munitions factory in Bolton and came home at regular intervals. It did mean that there was a little more space for the rest of us in the two up and two down council house that was 8 Elm Terrace. Grandma had the front bedroom and we children shared the back bedroom with Mum. Frank Loughran was Ella's man and had been for a long time much to Mum's exasperation. The 'engagement' had gone on for a long time because he was a Catholic and we were Protestants. There were unspoken (to us children) objections chiefly from Grandma and his mother. They didn't marry until 1952 after his parents and Grandma were dead.

I never really understood or observed the strain Mum must have been under. Indeed she shielded us completely from the horrors of the war. How she managed with all that she had to put up with and remained the kind and loving mother she was to both of us is a miracle. I can only marvel at her courage and strength and wonder if I would have managed as well in similar circumstances.

I have included three letters which Mum wrote to Dad when he was not around, some of the few photographs I have of those times, her shopping lists and a list of the books she read. I have also added a list of the people as far as I can remember who are mentioned in the diaries.

Bill Crouch
January 2010

DEDICATION

To Mum,
who desperately wanted to see a work
of hers in print. She would have been
so pleased and proud to see this.

I am immensely grateful to my dear wife,
Margaret, for her unfailing help and
encouragement in transcribing Mum's diaries.
Her patience, perception and suggestions made
sense out of Mum's terrible handwriting and
kept me going when I was ready to give up.

Where a word or its meaning is unclear, I have made a guess and used italics. Editorial comments or additions have been placed in square brackets. Those too long to fit comfortably within the main text have been included as endnotes.

I have transcribed everything she wrote in her diaries, letters and notes. Sometimes her indecipherable handwriting, impenetrable abbreviations and curious spelling have beaten me. Then I have just left a gap filled with dots. I think she would have understood.

1941

[Entries in pencil and difficult to decipher until
Sunday 9th March and thereon in ink unless noted.]

Tuesday, New Year's Eve

Another New Year's Eve my love without you, only your
presence in my heart.

First Foot was young Ivor Gill. Very shy but wished us luck
very nicely & cut cake not so bad.

Wednesday, 1 January

Happy New Year says Billy and Eleanor to everyone. Eve down
for tea with John. Crackers and paper hats so Billy called it a
Party. Mother's Ruby Wine tasted like jelly mixture. Decent port
at Mrs. Lax. Fish for dinner, M's meat to get. Far from starving,
Hitler.

Thursday, 2 January

Mrs. G[ill] describes RAF Pilot parachuted into Norway after
bombing Germany. Saved and … fed and sent home in motor
boat by S.A. …

Friday, 3 January
Bardia fell.

Monday, 6 January
Washing by Ella, I cleaned up and cooked dinner. Pictures at night.

Wednesday, 8 January
Eve's for tea. Ralph on night shift.
Memo: Eve's birthday and wedding anniversary [8th] either 8th or 9th.

Thursday, 9 January
Bedroom.
Walk with chi[ldren].

Friday, 10 January
Pictures at Consett. Spencer Tracy in North West Passage, particularly interesting.

Saturday, 11 January
Cold frosty windy. Teatime. Saw movement in Crosby's backroom. Ella hurried off to pictures. Just missed Freddie lad, David Winston Crosby born 9.30 pm.

Sunday, 12 January
Ella at Crosby's. Freddie lad followed her round all day. Edna always puts custard in dish first then fruit. Wrapped pipes in old stockings in bathroom. Very cold.

Monday 13 January
Increased allowance from Will. 7/- rise. Yippee. Feel quite rich. Wonder if he has got promotion. Freddie lad complains of insufficient gravy and shows Ella how to use washer. Reads instructions to her. Gertcher. Sent Club money to B[ourne]/m[ou]th 30/-.

Tuesday 14 January

Billy and Eleanor over to see Aunty but really to see baby. Wee hands and cot. Why can't we have one? Wait till the war's over. Tea at Eve's. John selfish with toys. Billy had to watch. John finally kicked game away so Billy would not have a turn. I would like to have him with us for a month, he'd soon learn to share. Pity Eve had no more chi. Freddie lad says Edna makes porridge a little thinner, Ella.

Wednesday, 15 January

Billy and Eleanor first trip over to Aunty before play. Teddie's now called David. Eleanor puts her David to bed in her cot. Says David has wet the bed. Freddie lad asks for cream cakes. Aunt eventually brings them out. Ella felt as if he thought she'd swallowed the lot. He tells her she can have one.

Memo: Find out which day bombs were dropped in Crookhall about 8 am. Five fell in fields. No damage. Never heard them Monday.

Thursday, 16 January

Very frosty and cold. Wire from Will. Outlet for bath frozen. Tank filling slowly. Burnt Primus stove and candles. Got it away. Mrs. Hardy frozen up.

Went to see Edna and baby. Lovely boy, very good. Wee bit envious. Comfortable home of her own. Margaret and baby not so good as mine. Ahem. Husband with her even if not A1 specimen.

Friday, 17 January

On News: German planes blitz Malta yesterday. Such a small island, effects felt all over. Got down to Butcher's at 9.45 am for Sunday joint. Not much meat. Shop crowded. Got Eve's ... up. Did well for Rations, treacle, 4 eggs, milk. Freddie lad shows Ella button off coat, stands till she sews it on. Kept candle inside 2 plant pots in B[ath] Room.

Saturday, 18 January

More raids on Malta. I am dreading to hear a knock in case it's a telegram, but No News is Good News. Oh Lord give us strength to bear our burden of anxiety. Still burning candle in Bathroom.

Sunday, 19 January

Heavy snow fell all day. Wind piling snow.

Monday, 20 January

Snow over 2 ft high at back door. Ella had to dig way out. Buses stopped over Hat & Feather, High Staples, Delves Lane. No milk today except from farm. Washed; dried in the house through the night. Mrs. Bell frozen, Mrs. Green pipes burst. Enough coal in house to last the day. Mother prepared to sit near fire all day.

Freddie lad reminds Ella that butter is rationed. Keeping butter for Edna, says Ella. We are using marge. Oh yes, that's right, says Freddie.

Tuesday, 21 January

Store milk round again. Ironed. Down at Depot for coal. Wore Wellingtons. Slipped all over. How do the women manage to pull coal on sledges? Sowerby brought ours on Lorry. Charged 1/6 for 3 bags. Makes coal dear 4/7 + 1/6, 6/1 for 3 cwts.

Eve down. Delves Lane snowed up over weekend. Mrs. Hardy pipes burst. Eve says put more down for Fire Fighting then will get Insurance if own is destroyed.

Wednesday, 22 January

More snow. Need big Wellingtons. Library.

Eleanor cold in throat. Rubbed with Vick. [Mum was a great believer in Vick and I have inherited her faith in it. I have a jar of the magic stuff by my bed to this day.] Careful not to forget emulsion. Sat with Edna till Freddie returns from freemasons.

Says he is much more considerate more thrilled than when Marg. was born. Will let her keep Ella for month. Ella willing. [?] And she is going to make the most of it. How is it that some people are so self-satisfied, so self-contented? They tell you that their work is good before you have a chance to approve. Show your light before men that they may see your good works. Maybe I expect too much discernment in others. I take it for granted that others can recognise good work. That may be wrong. It seems that if you want people to know how wonderful you are, you first tell them yourself. Perfect examples: Hitler & Musso. But who wants to be like them? Most everybody would like to be Headlines once in a while if only in their own home.

Thursday, 23 January

Eleanor's throat slightly clearer.

Wired to Malta at Consett. You will be anxious, said P/ Mistress. At Eve's for tea. John in trouble at school. Teacher hurt [?] … Eve addressed her as Dear Teacher in letter.

Friday, 24 January

General cleanup.

Shopping. Leg of mutton. Very good. Manager, no pies to three women. Showed the letter owing to weather can't transport them. Pies on my order in my bag when I got home. He sounded so convincing.

Eleanor's throat better.

Eve down for tea. Agrees with Mrs. G[ill] Newcastle machine gunned. [This last crossed out.]

Saturday, 25 January

Town with Ella. She got order to travel to Bolton Lancs. to start War Work Training. Lunch Carrick's. Steak & Cow Heel Pie. Hunted for Wellingtons for Billy. No luck, got galoshes. Identity DSS at WD. Eve in town also but never saw her. Saw grand curtain material fawn background gold orange mist brown leaves. 4/11 yd.

Sunday, 26 January

Siren went at dinner time. Mother saw wardens go past. We thought it would be Parade. She said, "It looks as if something's on." Man passing said, "There is sirens going." Chi at S[unday] School. Snip went with them and sat in class till the end. Ella left on 8 pm bus for Auntie Nellie's to spend night there. Frank with her. Godspeed.

Monday 27 January

Ella left Central [Station, Newcastle] for Manchester. Cold day. Snow. Washed lots of clothes. Bedding. Chi miss Ella. Eleanor went over Crosby's to see Aunty. Baby David distracted her attention. Frank started work erecting. [?] Billy's eye swollen.

Tuesday 28 January

Ironed. Tidied up. Still snowing. Depot for coals. Albert's boy brought cwt. Missed him to give him tip. Remember next week. In Mrs. Brown's to explain about coals. Nice home. Browns & fawns. Big window. Baby woke up. Billy and Eleanor tried to rock pram, nearly wrecked house. Home quick. Billy's eye worse. Bruise or cold? Rubbed round with Vick. Ralph down a.m.

Wednesday, 29 January

Bedrms. Library. Tea at Eve's without chi. Says E Thompson at Middlesboro heard machine gun bullets zipping along roof of shelter. What sort of shelter?

Billy's eye very bloodshot. Definitely cold. Bathed it. Dropped caster oil in. Gave him ½ Anadin.

Thursday, 30 January

Letter from Ella. Stranded in Bolton on Mon. Given address of digs but woman refused to let her in. Dark and snowing.

Neighbours took her in for the night. Work from 8 am till 7 pm. Home 9 pm. Organisation at fault. Bad start for young girls away from home. Why send them so far away? Cleaned bedrooms. Mutton chops.

Friday, 31 January

General cleanup. Shopping. Packed shop, 4 eggs, pies. Mixed butter with marge. Not bad. Use less sugar for my tea. Eleanor likes it on her bread.

Eve, John and Ralph for tea. Managed to keep Billy in bed most morning. Breakfast in bed not so bad later but no appetite. ½ Anadin three times.

Saturday, 1 February

Letter from Ella. Chummed up with girl. Dig with her. Dusted round. Library.

Sunday, 2 February

Eleanor wants breakfast in bed. Nothing doing. Billy lively enough but no appetite. 3/- bottle of Scotts' Emulsion [another popular – but not with me – remedy] at Store no extra tax like at Paces. Pork for dinner. Not bad at all. Mother up at Eve's. Grandparents' day. Nolloths there. Too snowy for chi to go to S School. Billy's cold heavy. Talked through all his meals to get out of eating.

Monday, 3 February

Not so good today. Wind, Frost Very Cold. Billy bad with catarrh. Chi not out again. Only washed woollies.

Pay day 5/- in savings stamps, 10/- to B/mth. Letter from Will's mother says Cyril gone to Kent. May be near Ron. Seems to think Will is deliberately not writing to her. I have had nothing since before Xmas and that dated Oct 16th, 40. Finished script. Siren sounded 12.20 pm. All Clear half hour later.

Tuesday, 4 February

Lovely sunshine. Chi out. Washed and hung them outside. Didn't dry but nice smell. Billy much better. Ate some dinner. Eve down. Saw soldiers parading with G[as] Masks though Tear Gas Van. Took coats off to it. All getting prepared & we don't even carry G.M. She doesn't mind gas but frightened of Bacteria. Soldiers been on the go all weekend. I reminded her of Big Manoeuvres reported in paper. She's sure Huns will make straight for Consett. Posted script to BBC. Nearly brought it home to put in fire. Frank down. Looked very weather beaten and tired.

Wednesday, 5 February

Awful day. Wind. Some snow. Chi never out. Very tiresome. Ironed plus usual work. Eve & ET down for supper. Enjoyed hen party. Showed snaps. She has a gorgeous gold lighter. Kept Eve off politics. Started on Communal Feeding. J.B. P[riestley][1] on Sunday night. Sardines on toast for supper. Very tasty, very sweet.

Letter from Ella. Not satisfied with digs, wants to be nearer work. E Thompson said tube of bacteria picked up N Yorks intended for reservoir.

Thursday, 6 February

Bedrooms, windows. Consett in afternoon. Material for dress. Pink bows & white check crepe 1/- yd. Should look smart. Mrs. Gill asked if I heard thuds. Lovely day. Chi out. Use old car … front wheels as snow plough. Got TE Lawrence, 'Oriental Assembly'. R[osita] Forbes, 'Forbidden Roads'. S[usan] Ertz ['No Hearts to Break'].

Sat up writing on Malta. Sent Parcel to Ella. Billy's appetite better. Washed their hair. Looks beautiful.

Friday, 7 February

Turned kitchen furniture round while Mother was at Consett. Looks more spacious. Will would say ... Shopped at Walter Wilson's. Rations plus 2 eggs. Mother remembers tomatoes 2d a stone now 7d ½ stone. Eve and John to tea. She does use some sugar 3 spfs to a cup. Decent biscuits today. John, Billy Eleanor nearly finish them. Eve concerned about Soldiers wearing eyeshades. Pictures: Dead End Kids, Good. Zoo in Spring. Lovely Moon, go tell my beloved I await him. Cat devoured 1½ kippers. Benghazi in our hands again. 6 pm.

5/- bottle of Scotts Emulsion. Billy ate double helpings both courses. [?]

Saturday, 8 February

Snow nearly gone – but roads very dirty. Swilled paths. Consett this afternoon. Lipstick scarce & rouge. Rely on the beauty of naked face. Children saw Eve and John in W[alter] W[ilsons]. She tells me that Frank has been hurt, in Infirmary suffering from shock & bruises. Walked home. Lovely & fresh wind on our backs. Chi very tired called for sugar. What a forgetting? Mrs? caught up with us. J Temple photo in paper for news of him. Man at linen stall wanted towel for prisoner son. Linen man gave him one. Crook? or genuine? Mrs. Calson in Report Raid in N/C on Thursday N/C, a heap of ruins?? Heard M[arie] Lloyds' life on radio. (N Jacobs, must read her book. Me again.)

Sunday, 9 February

Chi at S School. Tea at Stanley. Aunty Norma (Billy said). Bus packed. Eleanor became friendly with elderly man behind who gave her chocolate (dirty face) and let her listen to his watch. Good tea, trifle, scones, buns, sandwich cake, walnut cake. Then they dared to demand dinner with Mr. N at 5.15. Pie smelt delicious. Eleanor slept in bus home. Very happy. Tripped up with dish of water to wash them, wet both of them, poor kids. Up to bed, fast asleep in short while.

Been lovely mild day, fresh wind. Roads clean but paths still dirty. Listened to W Churchill. Invigorating. Malta raided Frid night.

[At top of page] Read TE Lawrence. Wish I could know the Arabs like he did. Understand them as Man to Man. Susan Ertz, 'No Hearts to Break' ... & Brother Jerome's 'American Wife'. Interesting.

Monday, 10 February

Malta raid Sat night. Civilian casualties.

Washed. Glorious day. Dried outside. Mrs Gill & [Salvation] Army S School. Mervyn no glasses. Can't read hymn. Should read at his age. No glasses. Should he see he has glasses. Smack his face if he laughs at me. Called at Daly's. Saw Nellie L[oughran]. Advised to visit Frank at Infirmary. Looked weak but better than I expected. Much bandaged. Fell 45 ft. Grand feeling falling but no memory of falling. Able to sit up & smoke. Ate some dinner. Nellie very friendly. Why can't Ella behave normally? If only she would see that Love and Life are more important than Religion & what others think.

Billy asked at tea, What makes smoke go up in the sky? (Wind) What fixed the blue in the sky? Was it off train? specials?

Tuesday, 11 February

Mother took chi to depot & up to Eve's. Dinner alone. Sliced potato & shredded carrot cooked in milk, cold sirloin, rhubarb, date & custard. Good coals 9d for 3 cwts. Mr. Barker, Mrs. G about SA Capt. & chi. Billy & Mother returned 2.15 pm. Went to seek Eleanor. Stayed tea. Eve says G[erman] plane at 6.20 in afternoon 2 Spitfires. Warden says no sign of it. Home 7 pm bed 7.15 pm. Moving some. Pictures. Mother matting. Mrs. Lax called this am. Looks bad. Fell in snow in yard. Lay 10. 15 20 minutes. Tom at table near window never saw nor heard. Fears she wrenched something. Awful pain in side. Cold, Flue. [sic] Fall of Bardia on Newsreel. Ambassador in Rumania asks for passport. Trouble brewing in Balkans. Will we reach Tripoli in time?

Wednesday 12 February

Plane round at 12.30, 1.30 am. Queer feeling waiting for bangs. None. Mrs. G very alarmed, Tummy rumbled. Cleaned bedrooms. Misty rainy day. Chi cross in afternoon. Pulled each others hair. Eleanor's fingers jammed in door (by Billy?) Our *cat* very fishy. Snip chases Toots. [?] Mother visits Frank also Eve. Stitched up Billy's cardigan. Won't call me Lassie Lad. Eleanor? He wrote letter to Ella. Thanks for candy rock sent yesterday. Gloves for Eleanor far too small. Letter from BBC acknowledging script. Pray for me, Lady of Disappointments.

Memo: Eve made 3 gill bottle of cascara, Gregory Powder, Rhubarb Powder, Oil of Peppermint & Magnesia. Three times a day. Busy time. One dose gave me a pain. Descriptive piece of Malta sounds well to me.

[At top of page] R[osita] Forbes's 'Forbidden Road: Kabul to Samarkand.' Must be a good mixer, Smells would put me off. 'Ben Sees it Through', J Jefferson Farjeon. Full of action & humour.

Thursday, 13 February

Easy Day. Finished Billy's cardigan, wore it for tea. Big but good fault. Rainy, misty, some snow. Chi not out. Played with Teddies' (David's) must sit them up for meals at tables. Eleanor puts part of her food on a plate for David. After washes his face. Eve & John for tea. Rumour that bombs dropped in Blackhill. Planes at 6 am. Surely we would have heard. Siren sounded 2.30. All clear 3 pm. Heard nothing. Eve said women heard Planes. Thinks. Alarm shd have been given more often this week. Men in charge must be trusted to know their job better than us. Raid on Malta reported G[erman] & I[talian]. Made off. No damage or casualties are posted.

Friday, 14 February

Cleaned kitchen & scullery. Still raining. Chi out afternoon. What a relief. Bedroom mats to shake because David had dirtied them. Mrs G[?] says friend reported Incendiaries at Whittonstall. Thurs am. Friend first went to her home. Known her for 21 yrs. She uses marge with jam. Butter alone. I was mixing them. Hurried down 10.30 am to get meat. Sirloin 3/7. Harry[?] 300 lbs short. May come. W[alter]. Wilson's for groceries. Jar of lemon curd. 1lb mixed biscuits 2 eggs. Washed cushion covers. Back on again. Covered with papers for Snip. Cat retired to sleep. I doubt she's had her fill. Raid on Malta again. Parachute troops in S Italy?? Cut up old coat to make Bill dressing gown.

Saturday, 15 February

Cleaned up. Keep off cushions. Swilled paths, doorstep, windows. Promising sky. Consett with chi to see Frank. War Bonds. Hat in Bonnells. Library. Tea at Hansons. 4.45 pm to Inf. Pigeon on Church Tower. Police court for bad people. Walked in. Frank home. Left Book at shop. Chi tired Bed before 7 pm. Wrote to Ella (documents). Posted. Searchlights so did not go to pictures. Mrs. G. news. Italy Roosevelt's Biorhythmic forecast. SA captain saved. Siren 1.15 pm. S[earch]lights over coast, flashes. Mrs. G. red star moving. Must be something. Cold & shaking with shock. Mrs. G. held door open with fist & letter box rattled. Heard bangs. Thuds of G plane or my heart? Glorious night, Jupiter & Saturn in Conjunction? N[orth] & S[outh]?? Bed 1.30 windows rattled. All Clear 5.55 am. News acknowledges parachutes in S Italy. Some not returned to base. Miracle that some have. Malta raided Hospital hit three killed. Billy dreamed of *snow*.

Sunday, 16 February

Heavy head this morning. All Clear 5.45 this am. Twice bombs dropped near. Reported Lanchester, Langley Park, Chester-le-Street. Mrs. G. tonight says big bang was plane on Lowfell. News says plane brought down N/c area. Very *big* vibration brought many to doors. Ee it's serious tonight. Alarm 6.30 & 7.20 pm. Chi to S School, 'Little children' hymn. I love yer *earthy* hymns. Eleanor chants round room.

[At top of page] Books. 'By the Waters of Babylon', Newman [sic – Robert Neumann]. 'English Ways', Jack Hilton.

[In ink] Persecution of Jews, their last hope was Palestine. Not a chance in the world. Accepted dreadful treatment yet did not organise themselves to resist it.

Monday, 17 February

Bulgaria & Turkey. Act of friendship. No washing today only chi's woollies & silk undies, socks. Snowed all day. Very wet roads. Billy not well. Return of Flue? [sic] ½ Anadin twice. Eleanor has tooth through so she's better tempered. Mother's big toe joint swollen & red. Mrs G. asks for marmalade recipe. No more news of Sat Raid. Pit villages bombed. Papers. P. Office 2 pm. Bought 4 twopenny *cars* and sweets for kids. Home. Billy very hungry at teatime. No tea tray on settee. Eleanor wants tray with breakfast in bed. Bed 6.15. Pictures, Warner Baxter [in] 'Earthbound'. Interesting theory. Dead man does not know he's dead for some time. Carries on normal life. Just what I pictured Dad doing. Weight fell off clock. Did he do it to attract attention? Finished dressing gown.

Tuesday, 18 February

Billy surprisingly well. Eleanor's voice thick. Letter from Malta, written 27.1.41. Says, "fairly quiet time?" Six inches of snow. Snowed all day. Cleared paths. Jimmy brought bag of coal on sledge. Together we could hardly move it. My hands! Margie made marmalade. Beautiful Jelly. Gave me half a jar. Sent wire to Malta from Consett. Hunt for foolscap paper. Small demand. Glad to get home. Eve down. Blythe Council houses destroyed. No killed but injured. Plane brought down, Marine Park, S Shields. Exploded after landing and killed some. 4 land mines at Chester Moor, two exploded. Some killed in N/C on Sunday.

Eleanor, Mrs. Crosby chops up some Potatoes for David (Teddy) Billy copies BAA BAA BLACK SHEEP. *Asked* Grandma to bake Apple Tart Rock Buns Scones. Snowed all day.

Wednesday, 19 February
Still snowing all day heavy. Cleared path three times. Chi out & felt better. Snow fell off roof. Cutting way out Nearly 4 ft deep. Cat? Dust? Burnt? Eleanor's joke 'Knickers'. Billy's 'Wee wee Baby'. Dusted bedrooms & stairs. Dinner, liver pot in jacket peas, semolina & pineapple. Pretty good. Went down street for cigs. Only get Woodbines horrible. Nearly crawled up Ridley's Bank. Wore Wellingtons again. Snow plough only been on main roads. Men plodding wearily from work. Some bus routes must be stopped. Snow up garden gate over hedge. Aussies landed in Singapore. No milk.

Memo: Letter from Ella Tues. Moving out. Girls think her Queer because she is T.T. doesn't have half a day for a booze. They have a quick one before work.

Thursday, 20 February
Started dressing gown for Eleanor. Still snowing. Drifts higher than windows. Dig ourselves out. Huge screens of snow at corners. Curling? Steep? ridges across gardens. Drifts higher than a man Above railings & hedges Narrow path hardened high as railings Like tight rope walking. One step off path down into soft snowdrift. Men digging road out behind Council Chambers

Main roads ploughed in village. No buses so roads must be blocked. P.O. shut. Mrs. P. in N/C yesterday could not get home. Piles in front of shops higher than doors. Narrow cuttings. Pits off Work off Schools shut. People walking on road up & down to Consett. Chi out this afternoon. Boys tried to make caves. Store with Margie. No milk again. Nancy turned up in father's plus fours.

Friday, 21 February

Snow stopped about 10.30 am. Lovely day sunshine. All chi came out to try snow out. Who can walk in deepest? No work yet. Buses to & from Consett at noon. Shopped. Mutton, Nestle milk, No store milk again. No bread or cake at most shops. Mother baked with assistance. Billy wanted to mix his own. Eleanor uses lav herself. Eve Ralph John down for tea. Delves terrific. Far worse than here. Walked for milk. Ralph's difficulty in getting home yesterday morning. Paid club up. Mrs. Coulson on back in bed 2–6 pm. Missed man friend. C. watched him from window but John's are terrible people who watch everybody pass. Pictures fairly amusing.

Saturday, 22 February

Felt under the weather. Everything getting in my hair. Row with mother. Took chi to Consett after dinner. Buses got through to Broom's Road Ends. Girl in bus held up at Flint Hill since Wed. High Stables terrible. Saw Tom Brown's Schooldays. Good. Then tea at Hanson's Home 5.30. Billy fell down on nose. Blood! Quiet night listening in. Sewed Eleanor's dressing gown.

Sunday, 23 February

Orders to dig road out. What a job but soon done by cheery crowd. Some grumbles of course said Let Council pay. Mostly women digging. Bad at bottom, needed more help. Alarm 8.55 to 10.15. In Mrs. G. talking after.

[At top of page] England's [sic – English] Way[s] finished. Good, practical, flights of poetic description. Fond of comfortable life himself but deplores poverty and hard working rules. How can this be changed. Three men & Parson discuss. What is Good. Church Canterbury York Westminster P. 1. No great riches? 2. Equal chances of education.3. Family safety. 4. 5.

Monday, 24 February

Washing. More snow but not much but showers on & off. Down street for Pay & New Book. Got 2d boxes of paints no brushes. Chi thrilled. Eleanor licked paints used finger. When washing I said Shake water off hand Don't keep it moistened Billy said What for? You've got plenty of water there. Pictures Sweeney Todd. Full house. Many chi. Roared & laughed at most gruesome parts. Mother finished small mat.

Increase in Butter ration announced. Start in March.

Tuesday, 25 February

PANCAKE DAY

Ironing. Arrival of Xmas presents from Will. Thrills. Leather needlework case for me. Téléférique Renault [a toy cable car] for kids. They wanted to stay in all day & play. Walked to Iveston. Clear dry road. Snow over hedges & walls. Lovely warm sunshine. Treat to be out. Eve down to tea. No coals from Robinsons for nearly 3 weeks. Pictures Sat Walked home. Flashes searchlights gunfire bursting overhead!!?? No coals from depot. Mr. Eden in Turkey.

Wednesday, 26 February

Mrs. Gill 6d for Home League. [A Salvation Army feature] Cleaned bedrooms bathroom stairs. Cold frosty wind & Sun. Mrs Anderson had Bring & Buy Sale. Took cushion covers. 4/11. Bought cake & glass dish. Plenty of fur coats presents. Cup of tea sandwich & Cake 6d. Good tea. Plenty sugar. Ada W. told future.

Long wait. She felt Will in midst of upheaval (in war zone). Not able to write. Opportunity to travel in Summer. Things will work out well by end of year. Young looking girl with boy of 4 (one at home 6) wife of officer sailed on Boxing Day. Letter last wk 32 pages. Miss Craig kept the conversation moving. Woman covered with fall of snow Lady present asserted she was still alive. Rumours of N/C blitz all wrong. Mrs. Hunt's Policeman Occupied Italian island near Rhodes. Posted MSS Malta.

Thursday, 27 February

Heavy raid on Malta yesterday. Dull fog & rain. Icy morning. Some bus routes closed again. Chi in all day. Alan down with motor. Played with Daddy railway. Frank down for tea. Looked poorly. Had friend to tea last Wed who lived round corner. Had to stay night. Mrs. G. told of rumours of 4 guards lost on Waskerley Fell in snow. Later heard it was 1 officer 2 men. Mrs. G in till 1 pm. Sanatorium at Ecklefechan. Old woman dirty bedroom every day. Son slept with Dalmatian. Maids out all hours. Leave buggers in drawer & lock it in dishes. Report in to Matron through window then go off again in wood. Housemaid receive lad in scullery after bath & in pyjamas & coat. Sparrow Pie. Mrs. Hall & Forster officers? quarrel over ball. Mrs F. Sunday joint 1/6 My we did enjoy it. Sewed nightie for Mother. 6.30 pm. ? said Man said Raid over? But too near for Siren. Snowfall. Asked McW. Forster asked First Aid Post. MO.

Friday, 28 February

Snow shrunk over 1 ft. Can see second horizontal railing & gate. Derek & chi dug path to shelter & gate. Shelter flooded. Eleanor used teapot to make 'Popeyes' (pot pies). Cleaned & polished kitchen & scullery. Eve down for tea. Says Raid yesterday. John sent home from school. Siren blocked up with snow. Some fire to make such smoke. But they sent chi home? L[ead] G[ate] Sch. holiday today no coke. Sirloin for Sunday. Still no eggs currants. Less cigs. Scarcely any in district. Few sweets. No pictures tonight. Boy said No Power? New Moon. Finished Mother's nightie. Trouble with dogs.

Saturday, 1 March

Showers of snow & rain all day. Dusted round. Started to knit green skirt. Exchanged 1 lb Marge for 2 lbs sugar with Mrs. G. Balloon barrage hut cable upset power house. Birth of Rumour of Raid. Dunstan men at works in shelter for 20 mins. Thus yet no Siren. Funny. Thought work had to go on. Teatime Billy talking about Planes Aren't our British Pilots best in the world? Do they go home? Planes into Aerodrome? Do Pilots go into proper house? Will Daddy take accumulator[2] to garage? I will when I am big. And I'll clean up. You sit in chair read book – And I'll put kettle on. Call me Polly. Still no pictures.

Sunday, 2 March

Better Day. Cold wind. Back door open all night. Snip with dogs early. Julie never called for chi for S School. Eleanor bitterly disappointed. Walk but not far. Streams of water on roads. Mother went to Hat & Feather. Wat [?] shone torch on 3 couples in bus shelter. Billy dislikes cord on D. gown. Promises to be a better boy tomorrow. Pulled out green trousers started skirt.

Monday, 3 March

Washing Day. Dried some outside Fine Day. Chi played at buses beside shelter. Feet & legs filthy. Another do with Patch & Snip. Four buckets of water no good. David's paraded in pram. Billy asks me to feel his tummy after dinner. Nearly five! Magic age? Eleanor helps to wash Doll's ? hanky. Mother at Eve's all day. Home for tea. MSS Malta returned, bad cess to them. Pictures Alarm given stayed in but maybe unwise. Home 10.10 pm. Mrs. G. long face. How could I sit? Planes over. Saw big flash Nearly blinded & headache. Snowing heavily. All-Clear 12.25 am. Grandma dressed before Billy can see her in new nightdress.

Tuesday, 4 March

Club 2/- General clean up. Ironing. Chi out & very happy. Billy heels out of both stockings. Eleanor long sleep like little Eskimo in fur hat. Dogs again Patch *??* in kitchen under our noses. Mrs. Smith makes good Attack. Eve down. Warden next door said yesterday afternoon Expect Siren tonight. Been on all day. Three German planes last night too high for S[earch] Lts Probably lost, Circled works. Mother hears from Proudlock's that Hepburn was hit last night. Three streets laid low. Saw women searching.

Wednesday, 5 March

Tidied & dusted downstairs. Cleaned bedroom. Mother did own. Frosty morning. Chi out. Eleanor dead tired but did not give in till tea time. Bed early. Billy discusses bulbs. What cuts them open? Eleanor's David wrapped in Blanket. Rediscovered dogs [toys] who bought this? Mrs. G. says F. Dodds has had son. Belongs to a) Guard after Dunkirk b) Lodger c) Lad she was going with. Such goings on. Billy saw Grandma in Nightie this morning. Up first. Finished Eleanor's green skirt. Looks well. Letter from Joan. Cyril had leave. She is in GPO.

Thursday, 6 March

Day out. Consett. Chi ready first. Leave gloves in house. Don't touch snow. Eleanor of course put gloves on & dirtied them in wet, muddy snow & rubbed her face with them. Billy wanted lav. So we had to wait for him. No cigs in Leadgate. Watched women with prams full of coal from depot. Where's our pram now? Consett G.P.O. for Wire to Will. Eleanor shouts in Want pooh pooh! WW no biscuits only one kind of sweets. Eve's. Such a dinner Chips mutton Herring roes Biscuits. Lovely dog Judy. Eleanor afraid but Billy loved her. Home 6.30. Bed. Billy wanted to take Teddy & dog. Siren 8.20 pm. Till 10.40 pm. Loud gunfire. Mother at Annfield. Sheltered indoors. Man put his face beside hers down the street. Thought he knew her. Never too late. Letter from Grandma Crouch.

Friday, 7 March

Cleaned & polished kitchen, scullery & pantry. Swilled paths filthy. MSS letter returned with thanks. Will try once more. No dogs around. Snip must be out of fashion. Lovely sirloin for Sunday. 2 eggs decent biscuits. Dates Cauliflower 10d!! Pictures On the Air Roy Fox always smiling Betty Astell very sweet. Eve & John down for the butcher. Rough house with lads.

[In ink] Only 3 pkts cigs. Few in district. Many sweet shops closed.

Saturday, 8 March

Misty rainy very cold. Mr Baxter here early. Talks of progress made between his grandmother & himself. 1lb butter for fortnight for family second ½ lb not cut into till next Mon. Stone floor to scrub. Half carriage wheel for fender. Sandstoned hearth. Hard work. Few clothes. His own house comfortable more food more clothes. Women smoking. Thee loser? against? it. Pithead baths. Where's thee wife to wash? Get thee sen a bath in the house and never mind pithead baths. Consett Library. Tray cloth to embroider. Up street afternoon with chi. Lettuce 9d. Cress 4½d Rhubarb 4½d Am dying to have a bit of think for Billy. Finished pinny for Eleanor. Cut her hair & washed it. Could not keep still Much shorter than I wanted

Sunday, 9 March

Dinner Sirloin Y[orkshire] Pudding cauliflower mashed potatoes, rice pudding rhubarb & dates. Very Good. Eleanor went to S Sch. Billy awkward Got cold again.

Cold wind. Frank's sister called for him 6 pm. But he was not here. Listened to Hi Gang. Forces Station very faint. JB Priestley not very helpful in a practical way. What can a Woman with Children do to help relieve her life? Can't go out to work, can't go to amusements unless someone stops with chi or else she takes them. Live day to day try to ignore War & restrictions. Live solely for chi but that's no companionship. My life seems locked up inside me that keep busy with little things while the Biggest Events in History happen.

[Entries hereafter in ink unless noted otherwise]

[Top of page] 'Journal of K[atherine] Mansfield'. Colourful. Poetic. Troubled with illness & much pain. So much to write about, so short a time. Born Beauchamp. Who was her husband? Close observation of everything even animals. Never content with her work.

Monday, 10 March

Cold wind fog and rain. Billy very hoarse. Play in bedroom. Cot is a boat. David's & dogs with them. H.W. bottles & shoes for fish Result of fishermen story. Billy very good Wrote two letters Ella & Gay. Painted book. Eleanor sopping book. Water all over table. Writes in shorthand. Looked over Eleanor's summer frocks All too short. Billy's 2 linen trousers not bad. Petticoats too short. Start saving. N. Davison in Malta been frightened of Dive Bombers Getting used & fighting back. Insurance Man elderly dancer 'teaches' the girls to rumba. Pictures nothing special but a wee laugh. Mrs. G. with Mother. Clipping clouts for mat. Bulbs showing in garden. Croci, hyacinths, daffs. House tulips like leeks.

Tuesday, 11 March

Better day but still damp. Washed sheets nightwear thicker things yesterday. Dried last night. (Feel of water, soft warm, foaming lather) Today pinnies, etc. Ironed tonight. Chi out this morning. Billy returned with pram thick with mud. Scrubbed hankies tea towel. Coals from depot. Lad with big trolley barrow.

Wheel came off in street. Match to hold it on. Heavy work. Eve down. Tale of Judy. Will bark. Woke Ralph up. Brought it in kitchen & sat up with it. Next day Eve belts it for barking (Key in one hand, belt in other) Judy bolted, leapt over gate up street. Swore up at R. Followed with leather J. round corner, crawled home on her belly. Seaside trip when War over. Sandwiches. At bedtime talk of trip to B/mth. Father Xmas. Rather have Daddy than toys. Can't he be a sort of F. Xmas. Billy doesn't want to miss presents.

Wednesday, 12 March

Club 1/- Wind dry roads. Mother finds one yellow crocus peeping up. Billy brought Barry & Alan to see it. Snow receding but still covers much garden. Freed small privet border. No cigs. Pictures New Moon. Very glamorous. Eve's for tea. No sugar but cigs. Ralph gave girl such a clinch, slipped 2/- in her hand & she said Well I think I'd better have a packet. Stratagem also got him a packet. Mrs. Gill in tonight. Talk on MEN. Newspaper man who came to see her when kids in bed. It's more than my life's worth to go out that door now. *Ben* wringing with sweat. Hubby said Won't ask any more You can ask. *Wreck,* 4 am. finds him smoking with light on. Can't sleep unless – You should know if I'm wearing anything or not. You say it makes no difference seven weeks ill, lost all desire. When am finished with that am finished altogether. Mrs. Forster every night and Sunday afternoon. Thrill to hear her on the stairs.

Memo: Siren at 10.30 pm. Plane 10.40 pm. Clear night, clouds high. Billy breaks lid of tureen. Told lie. Will Pinocchio's fairy make his nose grow? Yes. Well she doesn't know She's not here.

Thursday, 13 March

Glorious Spring Day Very Warm Sun Clear Sky. Chi out all day. Took Snip out on leader. Cleaned up kitchen. Made dinner Pink pudding for Billy. Thought he would burst. Cleaned bedrooms Sunshine showed up winter dust. Must start to Spring clean soon. Back bedroom a sun trap. Rested there. Felt sun thawing my stiff bones. Bath. Eve down with John. Mrs. Lax in. Bought her first packet of 'tabs' at McA[loons]. Eve & I got 20 Capstan each. Siren 8.45 pm. Mrs. Coulson up. Stayed till 1 am. Talk of last war; Food; Wrecked plane at Lond Hill; Mottee the Cook; Becker her man; *glyning* women sponge pudding. Bed 2 am. All Clear 4.20 am. Walk up Park with Hannah L. Watched shell bursts in sky. Planes passed over here on way out? Bit of sewing Here he is again. Few more button hole stitches. Left chi in bed.

Friday, 14 March

Glorious Day again. Patches of dirty snow spoilt illusion of Summer. Chi revelled in sun. Eleanor took high hand with Colin. Five croci showing their heads. Two purple primula unfolding. Snip content to lie in sun at doorstep. Cleaned kitchen & Scullery & pantry. Frank & Ralph for tea. F. got job at Hetton-le-Hole on Relay Wireless. R. in shelter most of last night.

W. Wilson's for groceries. Used printed Ration Card. 1 tin milk, 1 lb Jam, 2 eggs, 30 cigs. ¼ lb cheese, ¾ lb butter double ration started. Wanless short of meat again. 2½lb pork. None for tomorrow. Reports of damage at Bolden & W. Hartlepool. Heard at Middlesbrough. Plane brought down. Rumour says planes passed on way to Clydeside. Awful bangs tonight. Lobblely Hill gun [?] Went to bed at 2 am. All Clear 2.15–20 am. Alarm later 5-ish to 6-ish. Finished M.S.S. letter.

Saturday, 15 March

Dickory Dickory Dock. The mouse ran up the Clock To fetch a pail of water. Clocks in Jewellers. Watch strap Shoes for Bill. Material for Eleanor frock. Ribbon. No red ribbon scarlet wool or blue. Another beautiful day but still traces of snow. Crocuses showing plainly now. Eve & John down for dinner. Account of Thurs Raid. Planes right over 8 Pixley Dell. She hung onto mantelpiece & said her prayers. The buggers flew round works. Lively 15 mins. Rather have blitz bombs. [?] Frightened like hell. Better if there had been something to do. Incendiaries. S[tirrup]. Pump at front door. Ralph lost 2 nights work. Fire watching & patrolling. cold job. Ride to Durham in bus. Lovely. Lambs. Ploughed fields black/brown light & dark, one limed like snow. Lot turned under first time for many years. Hedges cut. Some fields lightly powdered with new green shoots. Too many people in Durham. Bill nearly Knocked down by car. Poor tea. No Siren yet. 11 pm. Bed.

Memo: Mrs. Coulson up in morning. Beck is very quiet. Next door without sugar no money. Asked for jam for Man after long shift. He boasts of £7 a week. Must boil it on fire & sups it? Neither inside them or on their backs. Always on the cadge.

Sunday, 16 March

Warm Spring Day again. Crocuses full out & primula. Mother in bed till 11 am. Cold. Lovely dinner. Pork. Thoughts of you dear. Met chi from S School Were snowdrops on father's grave. 'Granddad's gravy' Billy If these fragile blossoms can survive & endure such a hard winter surely we can live through these dark days and when our Sun shines again, dance out in radiance (Hopeless). Eleanor fell down in clarts [mud]. Ruined coat. Extra 2 bottles milk to make up store who got none. Forces programme comes in better. Listened to Hi Gang & variety at 8 pm. Scarlet Pimpernel decent. Mother dozing all night. Not well. Eleanor filled bucket of coal & carried in ? part full. Bill will not sit up & lift cup up at tea. Suspect he has watched Alan & Co guzzling & gobbling. Discover crocus closes at night.

[At top of page] 'Testament of Friendship', Vera Brittain. W.H. [Winifred Holtby] Wonderful personality, generous? Help to all. Early environment good. Sensible understanding mother. High School Scarborough. Later Somerville. Waac [Women's Army Auxiliary Corps] in Great War, saw shelling. Keen interest in League of Nations & S. African natives. Many living contacts. Varied & full life. Cheated of time to write.

Monday, 17 March

White frosty early. Misty & damp all day till evening Wind getting up Very cold. Raw day. Mother still poorly. Only washed few things by hand, silks & woollens. Up street for pay, another War S[avings] Certificate. Five now. Bought material for 2 frocks for Eleanor print & gingham. Stuff for blouse. Stockings 3/11 only semi-fashioned. Bill noisy & defiant all day. Difficult to manage. Eleanor just as bad. Pictures. Mrs. Coulson up beside Mother. Siren 8.35 pm. Come out from cinema. Mrs. Gill came in. Mrs. Breen baby girl. Never knew. Lives nearly opposite. All Clear tennish. Dark night. Posted MSS. Letter to my love. What a hope! Better to aim at a star, I suppose. May grasp a grain of sand. That would be something.

Tuesday, 18 March

Letter from Ella. Dry cold day. Washed. Line's in back garden first time for ages. Washed the Rinso way. Not bad at all but ruined vests pyjamas E. knickers by boiling with E. blue knicks. Shd have known better. Chi out the whole day. Glowing with fresh air spirits. Play with Mavis sand. Barry J. hit Mavis on head. Mavis hit Barry on the back. Bring firewood – big broken twigs & branches. Where from? Coal from Depot. Mother lot better Up at Eve's. Down after tea. Harry only has fat chops. No good. Ralph off work with cold. Manoeuvres Lanchester Vale Listened to bangs all day. Never heard all clear last night. Eve fell over bushes with Judy. Wedding ring cut her hand. Blasts – Ralph underfed & over tired?? So many things he won't eat. Ironed after chi gone to bed. Started to read 'Testament of Friendship'. Interesting.

Wednesday, 19 March

Club. Alarm at 1–2 am to 3.30 am. Stayed in bed. Never heard All Clear. Fine Day. Intended to clean front bedroom but kicked. Chi out all morning. Mother washed bedding. Given herself more cold. Will not submit herself to age. Cut out blouse in morning. Machined it at night. Went to Eve's afternoon. Eleanor still keeps away from Judy. Speaks to her at safe distance. Ralph at work today. Home Guard, R. turned out in deep snow to guard Ammunition Dump. Loads rifle with cartridges Other guard said Hi Lad What ye doin' Is yours not loaded? No. A'm gwan round th'other side. Making site for gun at Carrhouse. Digging trench for H.G. near N. Garage. Ride to & from Consett in 'Yarmy' Bus' [Y. Army? – Yellow Army Bus] Camouflaged yellow bus. Thrills. Billy understands milk goes down to his legs & makes them grow The rest goes to his wee wee.

Memo: Mrs Coulson in *?* of little stiff built fellow Lived at Hills. Wife went sort of queer Died away & buried her there. Not long since. Ay its no time since Ye never guess? who'da saw him with Tommy Vipond's widder. He goes down in front of me & meets her & they have a talk & he lucks at his watch & off they go to Consett together. And after all the fuss she made when Tommy went. She'd never get over it. Mind she'll never get a better man. He was a good man was T.V. By it's time as ah was having meself a woman. Said better have one of Becky's? Pears coming home this morning very late nearly fell over man sitting in corner on the wall. Ye'd better get home. What the B[loody] H[ell] d'ye want to be setting there at this time of night.

Thursday, 20 March

Letter from George & Queen. Letter & book from Ella.

Fine Day. Chi out as usual. Favourite spot this week is in field beside Council Chambers playing with sand fallen out of bags underneath window. Eleanor came home for spoons. Ran home alright when Siren sounded 11-ish. Busy making date roly poly. All Clear 15–20 mins later. Cleaned bedrooms, bathr[oom] & stairs. Very dusty again. Pantry after tea. Mrs. (Grandma) Crosby & sister over for half an hour. Looked very well. Sister nervy in raids. Ill in bed but got out to sit by fire. Had four or five cups of tea with a wee drop o' toddy in. "Well, we had to keep our nerves steady." "Get it while we can & when we can't get that we'll get something else." Chi very tired. Eleanor cut knee. Very lame. Tried the slip stitch step with bad leg stiff but found it too much trouble. Bed early. Finished blouse. Buttonholes very tedious job. Pleased with it.

Friday, 21 March

Cold, Windy, Showery. Cleaned kitchen & scullery. Dirty dog & cat. Shopped after tea. Tin of salmon 1 lb dates. Not bad. Assis[tant]. forgot to add on ¼ lb corned beef. Must be after him early tomorrow morning. Got 20 cigs at Hopper's Let Mrs. Gill have ¼ of cheese. Pictures W. Pidgeon as N[ick] Carter not bad. Feel very tired tonight. Frustrated love no doubt. The way of millions? When will this ever end? Bill says who put Oranges on Trees? Does God take this into factories? Well we must put God into factories I suppose. This age is a Machine Age.

Saturday, 22 March

Book Club March book arrives. 'Nanking Road' – Vicki Baum. Better day but still windy. Tea Man still forgotten Ella's coupons. Letter from Ella. Not changed rooms. Woman couldn't 'do' with their hours. Will keep Bill's letters till he is 14 yrs old to show.

Consett this morning. Tried coats on Bill. Harris Tweed 28/6. Golden Mustard 17/11 but could not fancy him in that colour for a coat. Lassie Lad . Got scarlet wool for Eleanor cardigan. Mother off to town. Cleaned up. Cleaned silver after dinner. Eve down with John. Obtained half doz eggs from Mr. Coates [market] by fair means or foul. He thought she knew him. Spoke as if I had lived with him for 20 years. Also got rations for 2 instead of one and daren't breathe a word. Walked home instead of waiting for bus in case they sent after her. Bill said to Eleanor in bed this am. "If ya should a laff I'll put ya in the baff." Sound giggles. Repeat ad inf. Very patient trying on coats & not at all bothered when we walked out without one. Eleanor very tired. Eve says Judy eats those little biscuits like sweets. Gobbles a few handfuls and then looks up to say Where's me dinner? Mother at Auntie Nellie's. Got new puppy Dog killed. Eleanor troubled What killed it.

Reading V[era] Brittain. W[inifred] Holtby so fortunate in early environment, education, outlook.

Commenced scarlet cardigan for E.

Sunday, 23 March

Two daffodils opened out. More croci & primula in garden. Fine but cold day. Snow powdering early morning. Mrs. Coulson up after dinner. Willie in awful way yesterday. Going to die. Depressed by visit to sick friend. Dr advise good dose of Liquid Paraffin. Good clean out did him good. Met chi after S. School. Bill asked by Mrs. C. on seeing his green cap Had ye joined the Scouts? B. No A've joined in the mans. Frank down for tea. Brought sugar. Very welcome. Job best he's ever had. His own boss. Good Digs with old Maid. At tea Eleanor left jelly & custard. Frank wrinkled his nose & said Naughty Eleanor. What for? Says Bill as can't smell any fin. He brought crocus in put it in blue eggcup for the joy of watching it open full out & seeing its eyes. Written to Will again but words are cold things. I can't convey what I want to say. Bill asked F. if custard & jelly made man's hairs grow on their arms & legs.

[At top of page] 'South Riding' – W[inifred] Holtby, interesting. held attention. Such varied characters & each sincerely described. No dialect not even the humblest character but conveyed by speech. Sarah Burton fascinating. Certainly plenty of coldness & fear of death in book. Written but not published till after her death.

'[The] World As I See It' – Einstein.

Rupert Brooke. Lost his glamour for me. Too ? also.

A bit lazy this week in regard to Needlework & knitting.

Monday, 24 March

Showers of snow all morning. Cold. Only washed silks & woollens. Fuzzy feeling in the head all day. Billy awake early & very fidgety. Little fingers & toes rap a tattoo on my back. Brimful of energy & I must be growing middle-aged. He is very scornful at Eleanor talking to David so much when he can't talk back. Waste of time. Up to Eve's for tea. She is full of cold. Complexion does not look good. Had given friend 2 pills to ease her pain during period. For two days she daren't cough or laugh. Surprisingly cannot think of one item of War News discussed! Sensation! All three daffs in bowl are out. Very pale colour. Eleanor asked for Judy today. Rode home in *Yarmy* Bus again. Bottom of carrier torn by knitting needles. In such a state of confusion. Eleanor took off gloves & hat. Glad to get home without accident. Listened to Monday Night at 8 and the Last Crusade. Philip like Hitler awaited omens & signs for action. Eliza[beth]. secure in belief of loyalty & courage of her people. Those poor men of the Armada blown by the ruthless winds. Such waste of life. Yet life went on. Every generation has its own suffering to endure & to conquer.

Tuesday, 25 March

Raining all day. Miserable misty rain. Turned to snow at teatime. Covering an inch thick by 10 pm. Felt lazy all day. Mended leak in kettle. Quite an achievement. First job of its kind. Nearly lost my tongue doing it. Chi in all day & most exasperating. Billy exulted in the game of jumping back over & forwards way. Eleanor washed herself often. Letter to Ella posted yesterday. Delivered here today. Addressed here – must have been in a dream. Mrs. Gill's sister, Annie, beautiful big liquid brown eyes. Pale complexion, ugly false teeth. Oval face. Lovely thin hands. Quiet gentle voice but ironic Humour at times. Bad tempered hubby. Greedy. Re[a]d my cup. Wish in & 3 more than days but less than week. Telegram. Long envelope. Paper to sign. Mix with Crowd. Sleep in strange bed. Present. Visitors. Wedding. Meet old friend H. Letter from A. Granda Jackson came in. Showed Bill how to imitate chick with nails and sang Cock Robin. Consett in afternoon. Milk sour. No red wool left. Gone quickly. Pictures. Tyrone Power Nice Boy. Mrs. Gill in at supper. Mrs. Hume mebbe dead. Rechabite's man got £15. Billy Turnbull dead. Maggie Day always had knitting when they went courting. Milly a bairn every year and he's just a spalk?? Take Mrs. Smiths daughter into C?? Moist *eyes*. Letters. She says he's dirty but she had nowt on her floors an' ye could eat off them they were that clean. Nowt in her stomach today yet till Thompson came with the groceries. He still has his pictures & never has the pipe out of his mouth. Mrs. Proudlock's son joins up the morrow. Awful eater & bad stomach. Hannah thinks the sun shines out of Norman's behind. Woke up to hear him calling her Nan Nan. Went downstairs. Oh my God. What the hell are you doin' here at this time of night? Mrs. F. complained she only got 31/- for 30 ?, H. 28/-. My bloody man is fighting for you as well as me. You get your money for nowt. They've taken my man away. Drafted to the W?? W?? H. I only got 4 oz lard. Can't make b. cakes. Have got a bread loaf & sliced teacake & buttered it. That'll have to serve the bugger.

Wednesday, 26 March

Brief Spring ended. Winter once more with us. 4 ins of snow on ground. Wet misty day. Bill dug path all round. Eleanor retired early. Not so well, cutting double tooth. Very nice dinner. Liver Onion from Eve, Creamed potatoes Jam tart. Cleaned front bedroom thoroughly. Used ammonia liberally. Only polishing & curtains to wash. Grand feeling to look at evidence of own work. Shabby depressing dustiness changes to fresh, bright daintiness. Bill & Eleanor play upstairs all afternoon. 2 Teddies two dogs two dolls in bed. Dying to open boxes and examine things. Succeeded in impressing them with the fact that jumping could break gas mantles downstairs. Eve & John for tea. Thought that Chaplin left her with the idea that Hitler is not to be feared, only a little man after all. Surely that is whole point of film. Must go. Mother there this afternoon. Not very taken with it. Had a go at Mrs G. mat. Looks simple but really difficult to make ends even & close! She mixes her colours very well. Hard work, should be well paid. Bill missed Ann Driver's Movement Lesson.[3] Eleanor clapped? Marched with pram, ??. Wished I could have [had] teachers like her. Hard Method of Council Schools will not develop his personality, only drive him through class?. Not real education. Never widen his mind or enlarge his spirit. Dear Lord who watches over children help me provide a suitable environment for his growing needs so that he never has to look back on his childhood as the cause of his failure to be all that he could be in life. Help me to give him confidence; to train him to be steadfast, reliable and true to himself. But to do this I must control myself, my wild, ridiculous temper, my bitter nagging tongue. Send him back who will sweeten and gentle my life, who will teach me to laugh & cry and sing again, who will contact Me with pleasure &

?? of touching hands, of aye meeting again. Oh to feel once again that I am the desired one, the loved one.

Thursday, 27 March

Fine early on but turned to rain. Snow practically gone by nightfall. Washed bedroom curtains. Dusted & mopped B[ack] Bedroom Bath & stairs. Bill & Eleanor rather hysterical, highly strung. Easily cry & flung themselves into tempers. I must deal more quietly with them, be gentle. They are such darlings. Mother reported Lost Identity Card. Form to fill in. Finished S[outh] Riding. Most absorbing. Fine characterisation. If only I could write. MSS returned again. Ella found new digs board herself. Hope she likes it. J[Y]ugoslavia in hands of King Peter.[4] Only 17 yrs. More power to him. K[osovo] & ?? in our hands. Cheerful news. My knuckles are sore & raw. Must be the ammonia.

Friday, 28 March

Cleaned & polished kitchen scullery pantry. Swilled paths. Showers of snow all day. Bitterly cold north wind. Chi out in morning playing with snowballs?. Discovered two white crocuses in garden. Shopping in afternoon. Chi with me. Run wild outside shop. Forgot White Card for Rations. To be initialled so did not get them. What a sell. Sirloin for Sunday. Eve down & John. Said Butcher Harry had corned beef to take place of meat. Listened to H[erbert] Morrison on Gas Attacks. Then went to pictures without Mask yet fully agreed with him. No wonder foreigners don't understand us. We are a mystery to ourselves. Saw 'The Dictator'. Silly absurd caricature. No man so ridiculous as either Hitler or Mussolini would rise to power. But the final speech reclaimed the picture. If only people would sit still until the end of a picture.

Saturday, 29 March

Telegram from my beloved. Has received our photos at last. Keep smiling & all will be well. Simple but difficult at times. Yours forever. Why will people supposed to be friends suggest escapades with black haired Maltese? My own imagination is fertile enough. But I must believe. Cold bitter day. Brief blizzards of snow blown up the street. Chi out. Eleanor came in crying with cold feet. Played with pram round table. Bill must go out to find his appetite or would eat no dinner. Went up for rations also up to Consett for chi's shoes. Watched cobbler put leather round inside heels also soles for Eleanor. Quick accurate skill with sharp little knife. Idea for Thriller. Simple quiet humble cobbler never suspected. Could never enter into competition with Food Hunters. The female of the species is more dangerous! Queues outside cake shops Egg? Stall in Market. Must be because I have no Man to feed. But we don't do so badly without all that. Saw Frank. Coming down tomorrow. M Baxter & Mrs up tonight. Condensation? Cheese. Chamberlain Maverick/ £84000. farmer. Store Rations Ham. Jelly. Bill. Is God the Sun? Who made God/ Will he stop the snow? Where is He?

Sunday, 30 March

Cold windy day. Got 20 Kensitas at McA. Plus 6d chocolate. Chi at S. School. Cried again because boy opened window. Frank down with things to parcel for Ella. Accumulator run down so did not hear 'Peter Pan' or AP Herbert.

[At top of Page] 'Nanking Road' – Vicki Baum. Absorbing story. Such details, must be widely travelled. China, Germany, America, Japan, France, Russia. Makes immorality sound so simple, and interesting. Makes me wonder why I am living the life of a cabbage.

Monday, 31 March

Cold bitter wind. Sunny. Hard frost till afternoon. Washing dried beautifully outside. Wore gloves & coat to hang out. Mother at Store. Saw soldiers doing various duties with gas masks on. Asked me what the tube & bag were for. Couldn't make out what he said. Trying to get off with the soldiers? says one busybody. Billy & Eleanor out all day playing around. Cheeks like hard ripe apples. Saw Breen's baby asleep in chair very thrilled. Bill pulled crocuses replanted in his garden (bit of water pipe).Who made monkeys? What for? Can they bite? Pictures. Siren 9.30 pm. Mother alarmed. Saw flares. Thought the world was on fire. Very near, some say Durham. Mrs. C. up. All Clear 10.30-ish. Must have been lone raider. Snowing fast.

Tuesday, 1 April

Club. Wet windy showers of snow. Ironed in morning. Eve down at teatime. Had heard no rumours of last night's raid. Wonder! Got liver, mutton rack chops one kidney. Eve got sausage but none offered to me. Paid Club 2/- last week & this. Bill thought that table was broken & considered we'd better find another house. Explained that fresh house would be empty, no furniture have to buy new table if ?

Wednesday, 2 April

Letter from George. Covering of snow on ground this morning. Damp misty. Cleaned bedrooms. Washed Bathroom walls down. Pantry door left open. Cat ate half liver. Used kidney & remains of sirloin for dinner. Mother at Annfield. Heard bombs dropped at Lanchester, Manor House & fire on fell. Two alarms today – 9 am, 2 pm. Very short Heard nothing. Saw nothing. Announced Airmail postcards to Near East including Malta Price 3d. Good.

[At top of Page] Einstein – belief in democracy. Right of every Man to his own life. State made for Man, not Man made for the

State. Immortality lies in what we pass on to our descendants. We must never forget our debt to the generations who lived before us & gave us our civilisation, culture, learning.

Thursday, 3 April

Misty moisty day Heavy rain at tea time. Cleaned side cupboard & pantry. Eleanor talks 'dog' make believe. Bill joins in fun. Says it's died because Austen touched it. She also brought in make belief 'little girl' to play with. Two alarms. 11-ish am. 10-ish pm. Short heard nothing. Sometimes think I can hear alarm ringing to clear Valletta Harbour for a seaplane to land. Such a penetrating ring but not alarming like a siren. Plane landed as gracefully & delicately as a dove. Feel very negative this week.

Friday, 4 April

Evacuation of Benghazi. Germans & Italians advance.

Another cold day. Intended to whiten kitchen ceiling & take carpet up but feel rather fluey. Chose small shoulder of mutton for weekend. At W.W. got 1lb of B. Currant Jam No more this month. No eggs. 3 Velveeta [cheese] portions. Eve down with John for tea. Played Hell with Store Manager because Ass. Told her there was no treacle in the Store & neighbour got some. Also she got no peas. Bill announced that he was going to get married, buy table & chairs etc & have a new house. Thought he'd marry daddy or Chan. Eleanor declared I belonged to her.

Saturday, 5 April

Received 4711 perfume & powder from Will. Lovely. Gorgeous present. Bitterly cold. Mr. Hopper says there's a storm over Scotland as bad as the last. 'People's Friend' not arrived from Dundee. Eve down in afternoon. Had 3 eggs from Market so Mother dashed off Eve says she heard woman at Lipton's 'complaining' because they had not had a tin of milk for 3 weeks. She has had none for months. Is thinking seriously of taking rations out of Store. I took chi down to Store to see if we could get a coat for Bill but only size 2 and horrible drab cheap material. I do like a good colour.

Sunday, 6 April

Germany declares war on J[Y]ugoslavia. Advance on Greece. Covering of snow this morning. Very Cold. Chi wouldn't stay in. Must be hard as nails. Went to S School. In Church first Sunday in month. Bill sang & said his prayers. Eleanor kicked up fuss when brought in at 6.30 pm. I set fire to chimney. Such a lot of soot fell down. All clear by blackout time. Lazy day. Read.

[At top of page] 1. 'Dear Octopus' – Dodie Smith. Real characters. No need for more than conversation to describe characters & situations. Nicholas' grand Toast to the family.

2. 'The Lights go down'. Erica [sic – Erika] Mann. Brutally real yet sensitive & tender. Describes the conditions of life in Germany 1935–39. True facts. Country & town bewildered by contradictions & lies of leaders but still following them.

3. '[The] Polish Gold' – [R. M.] Low and [Robert] Westerby (P) 75 millions of gold rescued from Germans, brought from Warsaw to Paris by eleven men. From Beirut by Fr warship.

Monday, 7 April

Fine cold day. Cleaned kitchen. Carpet up. Whitened ceiling. Legs ached. Brushed then washed then whitened top. Looks better but not satisfied. More practice. Alarm about 11 am. Short. Went to pictures at night. Siren sounded about 9.30 pm. All Clear at 3.15 am. Siren again at 3.45 till 5 am. Planes passed over going North West. Heavy gunfire. But so very tired went to bed. Woke up to hear second siren but heard nothing else.

Tuesday, 8 April

Washed today Calm cold day. Poor drying. Rather big wash. Had to dry off over the fire. Ironed after chi in bed. Went down for Week's Allowance. Too busy yesterday. Got ½ doz. Chocolate eggs at McAloon's No face cream at Chemist's. No cigs.at McA. Caught Harry just opening at 4.15 pm. And got ¾lb hough [hock] & kidney. Lucky. Chi out all day.

Wednesday, 9 April

Polished off kitchen. Put up clean net curtains. Polished furniture. Cleaned windows. Fine day. Bit of a wind up. Dried sheets & towels. Dusted bedrooms. Mother took stair carpet up. Washed woollies. Surely now we are ready for Easter and Auntie Ella's arrival tomorrow. Siren about 11 pm. Lasted till 5 am. Dreadful. Worst night we have had. Guns made most noise I know but it was not pleasant. Very few planes over. Shields & Sunderland blitzed. Our Fire Brigade sent help to Sunderland. Sat up till 1 am. Then went to bed after cleaning every shoe in the house, trying to read to write & to knit. Felt quieter with children in bed. Such a peaceful little bedroom. Windows rattled several times. Fires started at Healyfield (Castleside) before siren went but quickly put out. Much damage done. Said to be 200 killed at N. Shields, Eve says Preston Workhouse bombed & none of the old people rescued. Another Report that Shelter of children was buried & their cries could be heard. Binns of Sunderland demolished, St Nicholas R.C. Church Westmorland Road. Roof off, School behind's worse. Once over thought Munitions factory hit. Series of explosions May be gun barrage. Never roused Mother or chi.

Thursday, 10 April

General dust up. Letter from Ella. Arrive 2.15 at Central. Mother off to meet her. Chi & I up to Consett after Dinner. Wire to Will. Secured coat for Bill. Blue tweed 21/-. Reasonable Smartly tailored. Mother & Ella arrived 7 pm. Been to see Auntie Nellie at Scotswood. Very poorly after last night. No sleep. Weak heart. Ella looks well. Bright & gay. Full of life. People she is working among vulgar, coarse, immoral hard drinking hard swearing but generous, good workers, smartly dressed with a zest for life. She put chi to bed while I went to pictures.

Friday, 11 April
GOOD FRIDAY

[In pencil] John's birthday. Ella up first with chi. Eleanor had doll to bed with her & teddy Present from Ella. Bill pair of stockings. Mother cardigan. Myself perfume. 2 Dozen eggs, 20 Players 10 Woodbines. Stockings for John. Eggs for breakfast. Chi in all morning then walk with Auntie. Up to John's for tea. Took painting set & YoYo for him. When we left everybody's arm was painted on & bathroom walls. Went to S. Army concert at night Stones of the Cross. Not bad for 2 wks practice. Could not get books earlier for place's bombed. Frank down at 8 pm. Been working overtime. 200 Relays held up for one man connecting up for free rider. Said that Wed night he had been nearly blown out of bed *? the ?*

Saturday, 12 April

Stayed in Sat morning cleaning & making dinner. Eve down for dinner. Lentil soup with dumplings & ham bones. Eve went up to W. Wilson for groceries with me. Woman complaining upset Mr. Ogle. Forgot to give me my butter No eggs. Box of cheese & celery. Gave it to Ella. Biscuits, Dog biscuits, baked beans, marg. Some pickles for Eve. Only 20 cigs. 3 pies Palethorpes good. Posted Easter Cards signed by Billy to George, Grandma Crouch, Gay & Daddy.

Sunday, 13 April
EASTER SUNDAY

[In pencil] My birthday. Nobody remembered great significance of this day till Mrs. Gill came in to greet me. Ella remembered at tea time. Time to forget it anyway. 35 yrs of age. Half my life gone. Only 2 children to show for it. Cold windy day. Ella & Frank up at Eve's for Supper. Mother at Mrs. Clark's Annfield. Ella Clark's husband Sgt. Major in Egypt.

[At top of page] 'Lovers' Meeting' by Lady Eleanor Smith. Have read theme before. Couple step out of 1812 into 1935, then back. The man returns to 1935 but she is prevented. Interesting. Is Time an illusion?

Monday, 14 April
EASTER MONDAY

Not a bad Day. Ella & Frank walked along Derwent. Chi played all day long. John & Eve down. All very happy. Derrick & Mervyn [Gill] turned garden over. Not dry enough to set. Boards in shelter wet. Musty smell. Picked Lorna Barker up, fell off bike, leg doubled under her afraid of broken leg but alright. Wire from Will with birthday greetings – My love never forgets.

Tuesday, 15 April

Did not see Ella. Off for 7 am. Bus. Fine day, Sunny. Some wind. But pleasant. Children out all day long. Bill too busy to come in for tea. New game. Make a maze of roads in dry earth & run cars lorries round. Derrick played at air raids & had ambulances, fire squads, bombs. Dusted & mopped bedrooms & stairs. Eve down for tea. Went up to Consett to visit Dentist. But took so long shopping had no time for it. Accidental? Really dread it. Sent Ella white lace flower for birthday. Started on Eleanor's gingham frock. Mother visited Mrs. Hume. Very ill. Sees great change in her. Slimming all the time. Siren 11 pm to 5 am. Lost nerve at 1.10 am. & roused mother & chi. Went back to bed 3 am.

Wednesday, 16 April

[In pencil] Ella's Birthday. Fine day but windy. Felt very cross irritable with chi when they spoke loudly. Bill calls me 'Mudda' Eleanor 'Mugger'. I much prefer it to Mammy. Think of fat black mammas in cotton fields. Intended to go to Eve's but the garden claimed me. Love the feel of the soil. Must use my hands to cover the seeds & rub soil fine. Set 5 rows of beetroot, 2 rows early carrots, 4 rows late carrots, 3 rows parsnips. The flat dark brown soil looks quite professional. Only hope the seeds do germinate. Mrs. Gill says landmine dropped last night between Easington & Hardon? Shell(?) went through S.A. Hall at Sacristan. Aircraft Carrier at Walker but sailed this morning. One woman killed looking out window. Siren sounded 10 pm. But am going to bed. My legs ache with fatigue. All Clear 11.45 pm.

[At top of page] 'Quest for Sheba' – [Norman Stone] Pearn & [Vincent] Barlow. The Hadramut. Rather dry, never seems to get down to the subject. Did not reach Shabira. Made no quest for Sheba at all but desert storms, wadis, the Starlight, well described.

Thursday, 17 April

Fine Day in morning, rain late afternoon. Cleaned up kitchen, pantry shelves. Went up to Eve's after dinner. Felt very depressed & liverish. Eve heard from soldiers who visited near Coventry at Easter that Rugby & Dunchurch are flattened. No word from George. Keep it from Mother. Best to wait a while. Letter probably turn up. Ella Th. spent Easter in London & had glorious weekend. Shops marvellous. Visited two Dentists after tea. Both out for half day. Toothache cured. Must wait for a week now anyway. Never heard siren during tea. Heard plane round through night.

Friday, 18 April

Not bad day. Rather windy. Chi helped to polish furniture. Chorus "There's a war on" when anyone went for polish. Eve & John down. Left chi playing while we shopped. Forgot Ration Card, so only collected extras. 1 lb date. Tin of Pears 1/6. Sirloin for dinner. Cauliflower 4d. 1 lb date, leeks? Feel much better today. Pictures later, Cowboy & New York. Not bad. Bill learning to play marbles with Derrick & Mervyn. "Go back to butts." Eleanor sick through night. Stomach too full.

Saturday, 19 April

Dusted this morning. Rather misty moisty morning. Cleared out later. Read too late that the News Theatre had show with 'Our Fortress Island – Malta.' Would have loved to take Bill. Wonder if he'd recognise anywhere? Probably make me miserable. Eve down & went up street with me. Rations 2 fresh eggs, ¼ lb cheese, also box cheese & celery & Leeks food, 1lb Palethorpes Sausages ¼lb homemade chocs ¼d. *Bar loose.* 2½d. Bar Terry Choc at McAloon's. Missed cigs all sold out last night. Alarm 4.40 pm. To 5.30 pm. Eleanor heard it. *Couly* brought 6 eggs first since October.

Sunday, 20 April
SUMMER TIME BEGINS

Fine exhilarating day. Windy but sunny. Grand dinner. Sirloin, York Pudd[ing], Cauliflower, turnips, roast potatoes. Rice custard (with egg) After Sunday Sch. Walked down Dene. White fields, Black Lonnon [Lane], Durham Rd. Saw Fantail Pigeons in farm yard. Pig with 6 babies. Hills patchwork of brown & green. Bus went over Lond Hill. Where has it gone? Has it dropped off? Lambs with black noses & feet. Palm, Bread & cheese. Skylark made me forget planes. Washed & boiled white clothes tonight. Save time tomorrow. Eleanor picked first daisy I've seen this year. Coltsfoot plentiful.

[At top of page] 'The Light of Heart' – Emlyn Williams. Character study. Father, weak unreliable, yet genius. Daughter, lame, very sweet determined to push father back to limelight on Stage. Robert musician wants daughter to take own chance of happiness. Father commits suicide to free her after failure to appear in new play.

Monday, 21 April
Beautiful Day till tea time then rain heavy shower 5 pm. Cleared later. All the washing dried. Grand. Finished & cleaned up by 5 pm. Set 2 rows onions 'Ailsa Craig' & 2 rows early turnips. Rain stopped me. 4 pm. Chi out all day. Bill found more Coltsfoot. Wild rose hedge in bud. Hope for more blossoms this year. Irises quite tall. Wish they were in one straight line of blue. (College Days) Must move some. White hyacinth unfolding. Daffs strong. Primula very pretty dainty. Silvery green sheen of dusty miller's leaves. Got 5 Woodbines at McA. Pictures "Nowt flash". Mrs. Lax home from Leeds. Lilliput 1/- pre-war 6d. Sent card to George.

Tuesday, 22 April
Club 2/- Misty Raw Day. Mrs. Gill brought me 10 Capstan from Matthews' shop. I went down also & got 10 more. Never been in shop before. Ironed washing in afternoon. After tea slipped up to Consett. Changed corsets size 27 but still too large. Measured myself in vest Bust 34, Waist (held in) 27; Hips 37½. Great surprise. Must have measured before on top of everything 38, 30, 42, Not so bad. Eve down Brought 10 Capstan Cold Cream & Powder (Rachel prefer peach) Alarm 9.40–10.15 pm. Finished Club. 2/-

Wednesday, 23 April
Bitterly cold day. Piercing wind. Parcel of soiled clothes from Ella to wash. Mother at Eve's in morning. Cleaned up kitchen

before dinner, then cleaned bedrooms, B[ath]room & stairs. Sun out in afternoon so slightly warmer. Chi wanted to play houses in shelter but still damp floor & smells. Eleanor had all her dolls, brush for floor etc. Washed skirt & 5 fine silk dresses. Sounds a lot but all originated in Malta 2 yrs ago. Mrs. Crosby & Sister, Jenny, in for evening. Terrified by gunfire in heavy raids last fortnight poor old souls. This War is a bitter end of a quiet life for old folks. Ella sent Cream & Rouge in parcel also T.C.P.

Thursday, 24 April

Very cold but fine & sunny. Bitter wind. Bill running in & out without coat or hat. Cleaned windows upstairs. Came down to find Eleanor under the table with tube of Tokalon V[anishing]. Cream. Said her hands were red. Cream on coat, face, legs, table legs etc. ½ tube gone. At Eve's for tea. Bill ate good tea but was very difficult & wanted to go home. Looked to be in for an illness. Fatigue & chill I diagnose. Had to carry him some of the way from bus home. Bed quickly with hot bottle & Anadin. Set 4 rows of peas today, also transplanted irises.

Friday, 25 April

Still bitterly cold. Letter from B/mth. Bill has cold in his head. Complains of ears & throat. Gave him T.C.P. on sugar. Swabbed nose & ears with T.C.P. Ate very little all day. Good sleep in afternoon. Ate 3 date sandwiches (very dainty ones) & choc cake for tea. Can't bear taste of tea or milk. Flue? [sic] Eve down to shop with me. 1 lb Palethorpes sausage. 4 Palethorpes pies. Shared with her. Ralph thankful. 3 oranges at W.W. 2 oranges at McA. Chi enjoyed one.

Letter from B/mth Mrs. Crouch sen. Short, nervy.

Saturday, 26 April

Still cold as mid winter. Bill somewhat better. Livelier & eating again. Gland in neck swollen. Went to see Gary Cooper in 'The Westerners'. Matinee. Disappointed. News showed blitz fires. Bill alarmed. Had tea at Hanson's. Bill made friends with hospital soldier. Sad & lonely. Eager to talk. Missed Eve. Mother out also when she called. Got size 25 corsets. Lovely fit. Letter from George & Queen. All's well. Nothing dropped near them. Another rumour. Cat had four kittens. Chi delighted. In cupboard as usual & on Mother's nightie.

Sunday, 27 April

Showers of snow all day. Return of winter. Black lowering sky. Set mignonette & verbena in borders. Hope they won't be killed by cold. Mr. & Mrs. Dining & Dorofy [sic] visited for tea. Brought climbing rose plant. Set it along railings to make hedge. Nice quiet friendly folk. Frank down also. Table full for tea. Chi played Hide & Seek. Eleanor would give herself away by calling Don't look & answering questions. Alarm 11–12 ish.

[At top of page] Read thrillers. Can't remember anything about them. Not even titles.

Monday, 28 April

White covering over everything this morning. Quickly melted under sun. Only washed woollies & silks today. Felt lazy. Read thriller. Went down to P.O. for Pay. Wrote PC for Will Air Mail & letter for Ella. Mother posted her washing earlier. Went to meeting with Mrs. Gill about Fruit Preservation Centre. Surprised myself by asking question. Felt myself turn pale in middle of it. Elected to Committee anyway. Feel very young & inexperienced beside O.S. matrons know nothing about Jam Making but willing to learn. Able to clean fruit.

Tuesday, 29 April

Washing Day. Very slow drying. Mrs. Gill had long talk about Margie trying for job in Consett Park to look after Games (tennis etc) Doubt if she has much chance with her stiff leg. Poor lass She is so anxious to be independent. Meeting tonight. Eve down for tea with John. No meat. Friday night raid on Heaton. Whole street of houses down (landmine). Old man sitting by fire with bairn on his knee had head cut right off by flying glass. Child unhurt. Still digging for bodies. Quick violent death preferable to life after War? Went to pictures. Nowt special. Alarm 10.30–11.15 pm. Finished ironing clothes. Best to be busy. Stops thinking.

Wednesday, 30 April

Fairly fine day but still cold. Cleaned bedrooms, b.room & stairs. Mother went to Matinee. Old Age Pensioners get in free. We went to Eve's. Chi played happily with sand waiting for garden. Stayed later than usual. Ralph unwashed after coming off work at 2 pm. Met soldier friends L/Corp Gregson & Charlie Baldwin (not Stanley) R.A. Pleasant fellows. Greg from Lancashire, very cocky. Charlie from London, very quiet but assured. Chi tired on way home. Mother got Eve some corned beef & us liver this morning.

Thursday, 1 May

Promising morning not too fine. Hazy. Dusted around. Eve & John down for dinner. Been to Butchers only got sausage. Caught 1 pm. Bus to Newcastle. Looked for suit or hat or shoes. Everything too dear. Suits 5½ - 6 gns. Shoes 29/11 – 42/- Came home with very little. English tomatoes 7/6 [lb] French Beans 3/6 [lb] Box of 6 strawberries 7/6. Only enquired price. Bought lettuce 10d. six spring onions 5d. Home by 6.15 pm. Mother went to Whist Drive. Afternoon beautiful Sunny & Warm out of wind.

Friday, 2 May

Wire from Will today. O.K. Fine day again. Mother took chi to Eve's. Work held up by 1. Mrs. Gill. Margie did not get job. Consett lass (cheeky) got it. 2. Mrs. Lax telling of raids in Leeds. Colin let her watch from back of room. Saw plane brought down in flames. "Flashlights If there was one I bet there was a hundred or more" Eve down for tea. Went shopping to W. Wilson's. Got rations plus evaporated milk 2 eggs. 4 pies. Small ham shank 1/- 1 jelly. Picked sirloin for Sunday. Spring Cabbage. Billy thrilled when I tried to set wave in his hair like Eleanor after bath ("Or me *shaves* out")

Saturday, 3 May

Left house & bairns to Mother. Went up to Consett. Lumleys with money burning a hole in my purse. Acquired light blue suit & dark blue hat. Admire myself immensely in these. Look young & Hollywoodish. Wish William were here to see the effect. Just what he likes. Tidied up after dinner. Boiled shank & lentils. Made salad with lettuce spring onions cucumber, cold peas. Did a little gardening Finished borders. Hope irises make a show up path. Eve & John arrive with soldiers 6.45 pm. Stayed for supper. Bill & John on Parade. Corp. drilled them. Just what Will would do. How I long for him. Not at all bored. Alarm 11 pm–3 am. Heavy gunfire but slept. Did not disturb Mother. Windows rattled. Mother thought wind had risen.

Sunday, 4 May

Glorious day but still chill wind. Clocks on an Hour. Mrs. Gill on about another job for Margie in Post Office cum Shop cum Housework Delves Lane. Good walk after tea. Four House Fields & Black Lonnon. Signs of Spring everywhere. Little pink pigs in fresh green field. Black winter silhouette of trees lighting & blurring Is it Ash with sooty black buds? Frank called. Did not stop long. Alarm 12–4 am. Jerries passed over. Awful sound.

[At top of page] 'The West Wind of Love' – Compton Mackenzie. Clever conversation pieces. Sympathy for Irish cause. Digs at Imperialism. Very little plot. Mostly political talk.

Monday, 5 May

Not very promising morning but wind drove clouds away. Only washed woollens & silks. Incendiaries HE bombs? dropped on fells. Muggleswick? Rowley? Couldn't get at heather for heat. Was this miss for Consett Works? Quiet day. P.O. for pay. No cigs. Few sweets. Went to pictures at night. Queue to come out at 10 pm in daylight. Alarm again 11 pm–4 am. Constant passing of waves of Jerries. Sounded over head, very heavy throbbing hum. Ears strained to hear whistle of bomb falling. One or two near thuds. Windows shook. Felt better with both chi in my bed. They never woke up. To think their lives are at the mercy of a little switch! Raid on N.W. Carlisle? N. Ireland.

Tuesday, 6 May

Dull morning but wind keen, chased rain. Washed rest of clothes. Dried & ironed before 7 pm. Mother went up to Eve's after dinner. Bombs dropped last night at Annfield Plain on games field near park. No casualties no damage to buildings. Raid on Clydeside. Mrs. Gill very pale & wan. Shakes the bed when planes come over. Alarm at 11.04 pm till 4.30 am. Wave after wave of Jerries but slightly south W. Not much gunfire. Never heard all clear. Too tired to stay awake. "Into thy hands, Oh Lord."

Wednesday, 7 May

Better day but still cold. Mother saw covering of snow at 7.30 am. Rain shower later more like sleet. Cleaned upstairs. Mother baked. Report of bombs at Knitsley. Eve down after tea. Bombs, 4 dropped two fields away. Heard thuds. Saw no fire or disturbance so went back to bed. Looked at craters today. Tremendous. If bombs had been dropped ¼ sec earlier (or later?) they would have hit Pixley Dell. Target Woodside Searchlights or Dump way up Humbers Hill? or just Consett Works? Alarm 1.15 am–3 am. Never heard it. Too tired. Nice to waken & find you have missed the anxiety and strain of a raid.

[At top of page] 'South to Samarkand' – E[thel] Mannin. Soviet Russia. Tomorrow favourite word. Shabby clothes. No individuality. Concentration on work output. Politics & Love their hard topics. Very bureaucratic but not efficient or systematic.

Thursday, 8 May

Not so cold, fine but little sunshine. Set lettuce plants & parsley slips forked flower plot. Lily of Valley shooting upwards. Dark red finger of peony rose pointing to the light. Up to Consett 4 pm. Eleanor fell asleep & kept us back. Sent wire to Will. Unhelpful female in P.O. – demanded what is an E.L.T. Down to Eve's for tea. Walked into fields to see Bomb Craters. Immense clods of clay very hard thrown up. Lovely walk over fell. Saw scarecrow. Man throwing white powder (Lime or seed?) over brown field. Picked daisies, coltsfoot, gorse blossom, heather in bud. No alarm.

Friday, 9 May

Fine day, warmer, slight breeze. Bill awake 6 am. Sick & diarrhoea. Overloaded tummy at Auntie's. Chips for supper! Eleanor demands breakfast in bed! Turned out kitchen & scullery thoroughly. Mother went up to Eve's. Called for new Identification Card but had forgotten card. Must go back. I think old I.C. is in the drawers somewhere. Shopped after tea. Nice English sirloin. ½ lb sultanas. 2 eggs. 4 pies. Tin fruit. ¾ sweets Cakes scarce. No Lyons or Scribona. Wonder if Lyons have been bombed. Pictures Thunder Afloat. Submarine chasers U.S.A. Last war. Good but … Never heard alarm again. 1ish to 5ish Heard All Clear.

Saturday, 10 May

Better day. Definitely warmer. Cleared up downstairs. Chi played all day with Seymours 2 girls. So slipped off to Consett without them. Got pair of navy shoes but unsatisfactory. Must change them 19/9. Also sweet William & carnation plants. Set them in the evening. Daffodils out, brighten the garden. Dug back of garden over old manure heap & burnt rubbish. What a smell. Cough very irritating. No alarm tonight.

Sunday, 11 May

Sunny morning. Black sky later but no rain. Garden's very dry. Vera [milk girl] say they had their own New Potatoes today for dinner. Only just been set this year. Very long winter. Frank down for tea. Listened to S.A. Service with Mrs. Gill. Written to B/mth (10/-) Alarm 1 am(ish) to 3.30 am. Slept on & off.

[At top of page] [RHS first] 'An Epic of the Gestapo' – Sir Paul Dukes. Easy flowing style. Makes even Gestapo men real if ab(sub?)normal. Lets really see Germans as men & women like ourselves. On the whole likeable, but badly led and terrified of the Gestapo and

[LHS] officials not always intelligent. Money still given preference over people. Soft travelling v hard travelling. Eternal queues for everything. Sanitary conditions bad.

Monday, 12 May

Wrote to B/mth 10/- Also to George & Queen. Cold bitter wind, dark heavy sky. Washed, all ironed & hung up by supper time. Last night bomb dropped on house in Sunniside. Somebody killed. Girl with broken leg shouting My new coat, Oh my new coat. ¾ qtrs [sic] of an hour notice of a meeting of Fruit P. Scheme. My address unknown. All fat, hefty, solid women middle-aged clad in black. Me lay low & said nuffin. Decided to see after empty house for H.Q. also buy sugar from Henderson's (Mrs. H.

on Committee) No alarm. Sound sleep hot whisky & sugar & aspirin. Cough a little easier.

Tuesday, 13 May

Letter from Ella. Promoted to Tester. Still windy but sunny. Not so bitterly cold. Third daffodil opened in garden. Strong, straight, superb, proud beauty. Mother reports row of seeds showing green. Forgot to take notice. Set 5 rows of potatoes this afternoon. Backache! But feel very superior. Used phosphate of lime 2 rows with it in the drills. 3 rows with it sprinkled on soil after planting. This morning sorted out large bundle of chi's clothes & sent to S.A. Captain for Jumble Sale. Chi out all day. Helped in garden! Bill wants to know if he growed in the garden and will the flowers grow big like him and if so where are their eyes. Alarm 11.15 pm to 10.40 am.

Wednesday, 14 May

Bitterly cold. Rain fell through the night. Showers of snow all day. The weather brings War or The War brings the Weather? Last War people said the heavy gunfire in France burst the clouds and affected the weather? Must we blame bombs? Two rows of seeds up. Turnips Thrills. Bill wants to know if daffs will grow as big as him. Was he a little wee seed? Where are daffs eyes? Eve down for tea. Mother at Dipton. M[others] U[nion]. birthday Meeting. Bishop & wife there. Returned late but I went to pictures.

Memo: The Mystery of Hess reported all the week.[5] A very fishy story. Everyone "doubts he doesn't mean no good". A.P. Herbert only alarmed that a German could land and be met by a shepherd instead of an armed soldier. Is he a Spy? Or Traitor? & would be leader of Fifth Column? Or Coward? North Mail suggests companions on his flight landed elsewhere.

Thursday, 15 May

Cold day. Windy. Heavy snowfall in afternoon but none lay for long. Cleaned our bedroom. Painted window frame. Took longer than I expected. Ticklish job. Chi took advantage & disappeared but not far. Next door cleaning kitchen & scullery whitening ceiling. They were thrilled.

Friday, 16 May

Letter from Ella, wants tea. Cleaned kitchen & scullery. Dusted dad's Encyclopaedia Britannica. Managed to do it without losing myself for hours in a volume. Eve did not come for tea but saw her in Butcher's. Sirloin 3/8. No sausage, pies, Lyons cakes eggs jam. But we are not in desperate need of them. Went to pictures. News Reel showed Malta Raid. Cried. Still a lot of Valetta left. All Maltese people. Strada Reale Castile Square looked alright. And I am left in this backwater! But it is best for the chi & maybe I will be better able to help Will back to normal when it's all over. May it be soon.

Saturday, 17 May

Not a bad day but still chilly. Parcelled Ella's tea & hankies. Gave bedroom window second coat of paint. Dusted around. Carrots showing faintly green. Granda Westhorpe asked mother for shoots off 'dusty miller' (polyanthus). Sneaked some of my purple and blue primula also. He was so pleased with himself. Showed his haul. Polyanthus on top. Couldn't reprove him. Age 80 yrs. Eve down for dinner. Visited Tynemouth, Cullercoats, Whitley Bay Heaton on Thurs. Saw little damage but she saw the sea.

Sunday, 18 May

Much warmer today. After dinner chi & I walked past pit along lane over fell through wood home. Heard cuckoo in wood. Glorious Gorse in bloom, daisies dandelions fairy larches, young beeches with 'lambs' tails', dainty birches, new light brown sticky cones on fir trees, sycamores with pinky buds pointing up to the sky, ash leaves unfolding. Played gramophone & Will's records bought during courtship. "How deep is the Ocean?" Bill not too well. Alarm 11.15 pm to 12ish. All quiet.

[At top of page] Undoubtedly under the spell of Adolph. Sir O[swald] Mosely married in Goebel's house. With Hitler & Goering present. Only one great Heil Hitler. Elementary Education poor standard owing to Non Party teachers & Jewish teachers suppression. Large classes. He serves God who serves Germany. He serves Germany who serves Hitler.

Monday, 19 May

Wire from my love. All well. Not a bad day but chilly once more. Washed dried & ironed tonight. Bill much better after dose of Syrup of Figs. Been very self assertive today. Aunt Nelly & Lily walked in on us at dinner time. Lily on holiday. Both tired after fortnight of raids. Scotswood dangerously near A. W. Works, so they will have to be on alert. Committee Meeting 6 pm. For Jam Scheme. Inspected house with Mrs. Turnbull & Mrs. Fulham. Very dirty but would serve after cleaning.

Tuesday, 20 May

Letter from Ella. Mrs. Proudlock's son taken to *M?* Hospital. Fine day. Mild & Warm. Washed 2 blankets, cot rug Back bedroom net curtains. Painted front bedroom window & bathroom window. Bill says he is going to work in a plane. But I can't go up with him as it will be a sholder plane but daddy can go. So Eleanor comforted me. She is going to have a big car and will take me with her. We women must stick together. Mother at Eve's. Friend went South for holiday. Had to jump out of bed & work stirrup pump in nightie & bare feet. House full of lovely furniture burnt out. No clothes. £3 to buy clothes. No good at present prices.

[In margin] Paid Home League 6d. also Club 2/-.

Wednesday, 21 May

Warmish but heavy atmosphere. Washed 3 blankets & curtains but began to rain before dried. Dusted & cleaned bedroom & stairs. Mother went to pictures. Eve down, stayed for dinner. Shepherd's Pie. On a hunt for bedroom paper. Could not find one. Brought 3 rooks shot by Ralph at Beamish Hall. Mrs. Gill suggested I should go to Home League on Mon. S. Army. Also Mending Party for Soldiers on Wed. Suggestion I should give a talk on Malta? Could I? I wonder. Went to pictures at night. Heavy rainfall in afternoon.

Memo: Crete invaded by Air Borne Troops & Paratroops. Their numbers are so great they have had some success. Our R.A.F. have had to withdraw because aerodromes vulnerable. H.M.S. Hood destroyed – News Sat. That thing of beauty. It made my heart ache to look at it. The slender grace & fine perfection of its lines. To say nothing of the grand & noble men on board.

[At top of page] 'Right Ho Jeeves' – Wodehouse. Brainless Wooster (decadent rich) in impossible situations. But very entertaining. 'Sleepers East' – Fred Nebel. Different American thriller. Characters on train journey involved in public scandal. Life threads meet & twist & part. 'Mein Kampf' & 'Hitler Speaks'.

Thursday, 22 May

Gardens look refreshed. Signs of peas & onions. Wish those cabbage & cauliflower plants would arrive. Dull cloudy day cold wind. Dried off blankets. Stewed Rooks for dinner. Delicious. Shopping expedition with chi. Not so good. Changed shoes for flat heeled leather shoes. Look very smart. Changed library books. Took Bill to Barber's. No trouble at all now. Loves the dash of brilliantine. Eleanor envious. Went over to the Welfare Playground for Bill this am. with Eleanor. Revels in the Slide. She went down it too. Also swings. Tried to swing myself but lost the Knack. Mended in the evening.

Friday, 23 May

Dull cloudy day. Some rain. Peas well up, Radishes, lettuce turnips look healthy. Tulips tall & strong. Dusty Millers (polyanthus) make good show up border. Purple black velvet petals with golden centres against silvery green leaves. Cleaned kitchen & scullery. Bill cleaned windows with old rag dipped in rain pool. Shopped in afternoon. Sirloin of beef 3/4. 2 eggs. 1 lb syrup. 1 lb Dates. 4 pies. Whist Drive & Dance for Spitfire Fund & Working Party. Score 160. Poor hands in second half. But enjoyed it. 28 tables. Dance packed. One poor girl had frock spoiled by sick drunkard. Disgusting. Had one Dance from Freddie Lad. Used to avoid him of Days Long Ago. Home 11.40 pm.

Saturday, 24 May

Siren 7.30 am–7.45 am. Dull cloudy cold morning. Mother off to town. Bill out all morning till 1 pm. Triumphant confession – Been to Store Hall to see Sholders. One sholder saluted him. Went inside Hall when it rained. Marched down Street with sholders. A little shopping in afternoon. Eleanor red beret & red sox. Bill white cricket shirt (grand) Eleanor Ball. Bill – Flag. Baked Eleanor's birthday Cake after Tea. 4 oz. marg. 1 egg. ([??]) flour sugar etc. Poor do. Looks alright. Mother returned 6.45 pm. Mrs. Crosby over to keep her company. So went to pictures. God gave a boy a dog. Beautiful dogs & scenery but highly emotional. Heavy rainfall in afternoon. Hailstones in N/castle.

Sunday, 25 May

Sunshine & Rain all day. Wire from Will with Birthday Greeting for Eleanor. Dear Man. Eleanor & Bill off in morning. Herdman's Farm to see calves? Took Bill's trousers down & smacked for shouting Not at me in the street. So went to S.School in good order. Both very cheeky to Frank at tea time. Eleanor threatened to cut his head off. Daddie will kill you. Shoot you with his gun. Frank clipped Snip. Quite a figure now. Siren 11.15 pm. All Clear 12.10 am.

[At top of page] 'Hitler Speaks' – [Hermann] Rauschning. Only his intimates allowed to know Hitler's real aims. The masses were influenced by his hysterical speeches. Real aim to Germanise the world and make the nations the labourers & unskilled workmen for Germans. The new religion would be the Super Man he would cultivate without pity, humanity or nerves of any kind.

Monday, 26 May

Letter from Queen. Eleanor's birthday. 1938. It seems so long ago since the moment of exquisite relief when she was born & I waited anxiously for the Sister to tell me whether IT was a She or a He. We were so cocky that we had done the trick and had one of each kind. "Isn't she funny" said William. He might say that now but with a different meaning. She's a lovely child. And was then. Rained all morning. Alarm 1.20 to 2 pm.ish. Invited the Boys next door. Margaret, (David couldn't come, would cry for his nanny, and can't eat) John. They cleared the table. Pineapple *p?*/cherry Bread (B&W) Teacake Choc buns sponge sandwiched with dates. Birthday Cake. (Tasted nice) Is there a War on? Later went to pictures.

Tuesday, 27 May

Washing Day. Morning not very promising but rising wind dried clothes. Heavy rainfall at 4.30 pm(ish) Ironing finished by 7 pm. Alarm for 8 minutes about 6.30 pm. Hemmed Eleanor's frock gingham. Garden tulips changing colour from green to flame. Billy greatly intrigued. Mrs. Gill reported at 11 pm. that the conductor on her bus had told her there was a German plane on Consett Market in a Lorry. Ivor & Derrick went up before breakfast next morning but found it was a Blenheim that had crashed somewhere in England.

Wednesday, 28 May

Cleaned kitchen & bedroom. Butcher's for meat by 10 am. Queue outside ½lb piemeat 3d suet. Got Eve's ration too. Dull morning but fine afternoon & evening. Quite warm out of the wind. Up at Eve's. Walked down from Consett. After tea walked to Knitsley. Saw may blossom wood anemones, sorrel, buttercups, kingcups, violets. Beautiful big beech trees. Chi fascinated by stream. Search for Dockin Leaf when Eve nettled her hand. 'Uncles' Charlie and Greg returned with us for supper. Greg going on leave next week. Chi dead beat. Home 9.30 pm. Disgraceful hour. Carried gasmasks in case of manoeuvres.

Thursday, 29 May

Rainy morning. Faired up after dinner but misty & very cold. Bitterly cold night. Wind & rain. Cleaned china cupboard above drawers. Ugly thing but hand-made by Uncle Joe & mother's wedding present. Drawers handsome. Chi spent morning poking into oddments in old pots & basins. Billy collected pennies and saves 10d. Later went out with Eleanor Took her Barry, Gerald & Maye down to McAloons & gave them each a penny to spend. Gave me 1½d back. Quite the Man. Committee Meeting for Jam Preserving. Lot of twaddle. Demonstration & Lectures Durham June 18th Alarm 5–5.30 pm. Mother 'matting' all day in scullery of all places.

Friday, 30 May

Dull cold morning. Sun broke through about 3.30 pm. but again misty evening (thick). Cleaned kitchen & pantry, also windows. Bill, Alec & Eleanor made mud pies in yard so had to wash paths again. Mrs. Gill in Town with her sister at R. Infirmary. Brought Eleanor a ring back. Little monkey doesn't like to wear it. Sirloin plus 1 heart (6d?) 2 eggs, 3 pies, 1 lb sausage (Cambridge), ½ lb currants, ½ lb tomatoes (2/6). Went to Pictures Night Train to Munich very good one of the best British pictures I've seen. Action quicker, but still one or two places dead slow.

Saturday, 31 May

Glorious day. Will it last? Feel enervated with the sunshine. Polished & cleaned silver Did a little washing. After dinner weeded the garden. Stuck twigs beside the peas, coming on fast. Tulips out (Brave Young Soldiers) Went up to Consett. Bought Eleanor coat & beret green (22/6) Not at all well tailored but passable. She suits the colour. Went into Hanson's for ices. Saw a Major at next table. Face familiar. Soldiers at our table could listen in. Said he was telling the woman with him how he was made a Major & life in Malta. Strange. Must have seen him there.

Sunday, 1 June

Wire from William. Not heard from me for 2 weeks. A Beautiful Day. Eleanor looked a treat in her green frock from Lancs. Bill was a Man in his first Shirt. Tickled to death to push the tails down. Went to S. School in style in New Coats. After tea had run down to Eve's to take the Heart I cooked with the Meat but not at home. I broke in my new blue shoes. Quiet day. Plenty of people on the roads for Walks. Rationing of Clothes announced this morning.

[At top of page] The New World Order would consist of (i) The Fuehrer [sic – Führer] Class, (ii) Herrenvolk, the faithful in battle who would be given large estates from conquered lands, (iii) the skilled workmen, the German Masses, (iv) the modern slave class of other nationalities whose poverty & distress would prevent over-population.

Monday, 2 June

Letter from B/mth. Parcel from Ella (jumper). Bitterly cold, foggy all day. Sun broke through 7 pm ish. Got up first today but Mother up before fire lit. Went up to Consett to send wire to Will. Just in time. Shut 10.30 am. Siren sounded 11.40 am. Came straight home. All Clear very soon. Did not go out in afternoon or night. Too cold & pictures would be crowded. Finished Eleanor's gingham frock. Did some mending. Started green jersey for Bill. Frank down. Brought some things. Been talk to Merchant Seaman home from Malta. Fine building down. Alarm 10.15 pm. to 10.30 pm. (about) Heard man in bus say that Sun manoeuvres resulted in Leadgate held but Consett & Works taken.

Tuesday, 3 June
[Should have been written in Wednesday's place]

Misty morning rather cold. Sun broke through before dinner. Glorious day later. Washed dried & ironed by 7 pm.

Cold misty windy day. Washed woollens, silks socks. Dried in house. Margy Gill started work on Ration Books at Blackhill. Eve down with John. Surprised Eve reading my card to Will! Went to Pictures Geo. Formby in It's in the Air. Not bad. Laughed. Eleanor & Bill planted forget-me-nots or bluebells in garden. Hope they will grow?

Wednesday, 4 June
[See Above Note]

Letter from Ella. Mother took Eve some meat (½lb steak) up John got scabies. One case of fever in his street so no visiting there. Hope he didn't leave a germ yesterday. Margy had a date but wouldn't stand on step to look for him. Not very Keen. Rubbed Mother's back, been complaining all day of it. Eleanor said this morning, Don't want curly hair so did not eat crusts. Bill off all morning again. Said been to Work. I thought the Pit but Barry Johnson says at the Snow Plough. Got ride home in Council Lorry. Thrilled.

Thursday, 5 June

Book Club. 'Night Rider' by Robert Penn Warren. Not so warm. Misty morning, very cold evening. Dusted downstairs. Cleaned Upstairs. Rubbed pantry shelves down. Billy up at Ridleys Field all morning. Roly Poly in grass but looks more like in soil according to his legs & trousers. Picked handful of buttercups for me. Went for walk over Four House Fields after tea. Very cold & windy. Picked Vetch [wild sweet pea], bird's eye. A white starry flower, grasses. Heard cuckoo & lark. Saw calf at gate. Washed my hair, Silvery threads among the brown! Knitted Fair Isle pattern in Bill's jersey. Nearly knitted myself into it. First attempt. Not bad.

Friday, 6 June

Warmish but little sun. Cleaned downstairs Shopped after tea. Eve landed down with John. I was rather scary but they had sense not mingle with chi. John gave Bill a sweet by throwing it on the ground. No sweets at W.W. nor eggs nor cheese but got some apple rings. Mother stayed out too long for me to go to the pikshers. Saved my money. Mr. McAloon let me have 10 Woodbines. Didn't care for the certain something in his eye. So many sorry for the grass widow. Alarm 3.30–4 pm ish. Heard Jerry then our fighters. Nothing more.

Saturday, 7 June

Coldish & misty-ish today. Cleaned silver & pewter, also brass jam pan. Shopped in afternoon. Cream cake at McA. Still no cigs & no sweets. No pies at W.W. Got Stockings at Grainger's (2 coupons) 3/6.

Sunday, 8 June

Fine day. Eleanor wore new gingham frock & looked sweet. We went to S.A. Anniversary & heard chi say their 'pieces'. Most of them incomprehensible due to haste, fright, adenoids. Eleanor took possession of a book & sang like a lark. Bill enjoyed clapping. Both said their own prayers at prayer time.

[At top of page] We marched into Syria.

Monday, 9 June

Not so good. Rain early on. Washed woollies, socks, silks. Down street to P.O. McAloon's still no cigs or sweets. No other shop with cigs. Have to stop smoking. No real hardship. Mother went to pictures. Started Eleanor's petticoat. Eve down with John. Not been to school but she says he is better. Did not stop long. Seemed to be offended because I went into scullery to wash up. She advised Mother not to keep frock from Grainger's. It wasn't worth 38/6. But when will Mother get a frock?

Tuesday, 10 June

Washed vests, bodices & Eleanor's pinnies. Good wind blowing, cold. Did not feel like big wash. Rather low in spirits & in health today. Went to pikshers. Not bad but not elevating. Ralph brought plants while I was out. 10 cabbages, 20 cauliflowers, 30 Brussels sprouts, 12 stocks, 6 asters. No onions or leeks.

Wednesday, 11 June

Poor morning but fine afternoon. Mother took Eve some meat up. So I baked bread. All by myself. That's the best way to really learn. Not bad at all, at all. The old hand has not lost its cunning. But mother will cling to that job as long as she can. She is the best baker of bread I know. Later planted plants. Chi around to help of course. Bill most interested in how why where of growing things. Why did God make caterpillars if they eat the cabbages? Why did He make snakes, lions etc if they bite & eat people up? Why did He make nettles if they sting? Ad infinitum. Expected meeting of Jam Makers tonight. Must have made mistake Florrie Vipond lent me 1/3 to go to Consett pictures. Saw Deanna Durbin in 'Spring Parade'. Full of pep, movement. Musical Comedy-ish of course. Got 10 Craven A at McA. and 2 bars of Fry's Cream Choc. Hurrah.

Thursday, 12 June

Wrote to B/mth. Not bad day, still cold wind. Cleaned bedrooms Bathroom stairs after dusting up kitchen & scullery. Nice liver for dinner. Mrs. Forster given job of caretaker of Palm Lodge at meeting this morning. She's a wiry, wee worker. Posted letters to B/mth (10/-), Bolton, card to Will. Planted the asters tonight. Did a little weeding. Was lucky enough to see Butcher's window open. Got 1 lb sausage, some for Eve. Chose weekend meat, pork. Mother took saus. To Eve but she was out. Sewed petticoat. Talk after News 1 pm. by officer from Malta. Ready for invasion. Please God no.

Friday, 13 June

Alarm 1 am to 5 am. Never heard siren but heard planes once. Little bit warmer Today. Cleaned kitchen scullery. Colds a lot better but they will run out without hats or coats. Bill discovered a pansy out. Not many pansies left in garden. Can remember great patches of blue purple pansies in dad's garden long ago. Lovely flower. No eggs, sweets, dates, honey, only Woodbines. McAloon's sent me 20 Craven A. Tomatoes 3/6. Mother got 2 oranges. Mrs. Pickering gave 3 coupons for a pair of shoes for Leslie aged1½ yrs. Very wrong. No coupons for under 16 yrs. Margie gave 5 coupons for a pair of tennis shoes! Mrs. Crosby in. Edna worried about Margaret.

Saturday, 14 June:

Windy but not too bad. Rain early on. Cleared in the afternoon. Mother went off to Town & bought nice frock, black & white. After dinner Bill went off to Welfare Grounds to watch Tennis with Derrick & Mervyn. Eleanor & I did a little shopping. No cigs to get. Took ices round to Welfare. Watched man playing bowls. Glorious situation facing south. Like a holiday resort. Started to bake bread at 4 am. finished 6.20 pm. Not bad either. Cut Eleanor's hair & washed all our hairs. Alarm 7.25–8 pm.

Sunday, 15 June

Very windy but not so cold. Hate wind. So does my beloved. Pork very nice but not so juicy. Went S.A. second Anniversary Day. Better poems. Chi had laid flowers on Memorial beforehand. Siren went but never heard it. Some say no raid only mending siren. Feel dopey today. Must need a good quick walk.

Monday, 16 June

A real Summer's Day. Glorious sunshine & warmth. Went to Dentist, Medomsley Road, Consett, had two bad teeth drawn. Never felt a thing. Made appointment for next Monday. In afternoon set onions & hoed half garden. Heat & sun nearly overpowered me. Bill helped by filling hole with water. Eleanor filled glass from bucket of water. She also tried to hoe while I was 'fettling' tea & uprooted an aster. Women's Institute Meeting at 6.30 pm. Accepted as Member! Miss Wedge gave demonstration of Shadow work Embroidery . Home by 8.50 pm. Maggie Tinsley held Whist Drive, made 12/- for Spitfire Fund.

Tuesday, 17 June

Wash Day, Fine weather, windy good drying. Big wash, all bedding. Meeting of Committee for Jam. Sat talking till after nine. Then ironed. Prepared for tomorrow.

Wednesday, 18 June

Not bad day at first, but heavy rainfall at tea time. 8.30 am Bus to Houghall near Durham. Lectures on Jam Making all day. Head full of Jam. Noisy unmannerly crowd but definitely enthusiastic Very tired. Home about 6 pm. Chi pleased to see me. Been good all day. Alarm 1.45 pm to 2 pm.

Thursday, 19 June

Fine again. Chi very brown. Bill rather off eating. Won't go to sleep early. Cleaned bedrooms etc. Tea with Ethel Walker [Mrs. Seymour] Eva Carrick [Mrs. Oliver] and their children (Ethell two girls; Eva two boys). My Bill couldn't be found to wash. Turned up dirty and refused to stay for tea. Gave out envelopes for Cancer Campaign to Park Villas, this estate then did Pont Bungalows on my own. Descent to Ugliness and Dirt.

Friday, 20 June

Cleaned kitchen scullery paths. Grand day. So many people wanted to talk. Work held up often. Shopping in afternoon. Felt like Saturday. Then collected envelopes in 6 pm. Handed in 7.30 pm. 25/5 for this district. Good considering So many out. One man said Wife was out and he didn't know where it was. Poor man. Poorly organised. Surely Leadgate would respond well to such an appeal.

Saturday, 21 June

Another warm day. Very tired. Exhausting week only got as far as Leadgate Front Street in afternoon. Ices at McAloon also Cream Cakes. Bill satisfied. Eleanor also. Pictures at night. Missed News. Germany marched on Russia.[6] Damascus in our hands. Only this week Russia declared our Warnings were just propaganda.

Sunday, 22 June

Fine morning. Walk terminated by most terrific storm I've seen. Thunder Lightning Heavy rain Enormous Hail Stones. Garden white with hail Rivers down street. Things in garden broken, bruised, torn, cut, riddled with holes like machine gun fire, flattened into mud. Lasted nearly 3 hrs. Speech by Churchill offered help to Russia.

Monday, 23 June

Another hot day. Dentist. Mrs. Stark filled one tooth. Not bad at all. I must be in good condition. Nerves better. Sent Wire to William. Posted Ella's coat and letter. Pictures in evening. Walter Pidgeon as Nick Carter, not bad. Told Bill to chase Butterflies off cabbage before they laid any eggs. Did you say laid eggs? Yes. Well, don't we want eggs?

Tuesday, 24 June

[Written in Wednesday's place]

Fine glorious day. Good Wind. Wash Day. Soon finished and dined early. General Meeting for Jam Centre resulted in presence of seven women. All Committee Members. So returned home and ironed. Members declared garden produce & farm produce ruined. Very little fruit here. Centre of storm here. Not even drop of rain at Lanchester.

Wednesday, 25 June

[Written in Tuesday's place]

Letter from Ella. Now Civil Servant. £4–5 per week. Not so warm, windy. Rain after tea but soon blown away. Dusted kitchen. Put clean clothes away. Spent afternoon in garden weeding. Terrible state. Much back ache & beetroot sadly missing. Early carrots scarce. Mending early evening. Finished one side of garden after supper. Gave McCabes girl head of lettuce. She produces chocolates Cadbury's Lovely. Mother had tea on Vicarage Lawn M. Union way. Whist Drive at Mrs. Lumley.

Memo: Barkers & Bells have acquired a couple of rabbits each. Bill watched their men folk labour at hutchmaking and thinks I could make one easily. He would tell me how it's done. I am trying to convince him that daddy makes the best.

[At top of page] 'Fanny by Gaslight', M[ichael] Sadleir. Victorian Days when every young man of family had his Mistress

& visited Houses of Convenience. Terrible light on the immorality in (?) Victorian prudishness.

Thursday, 26 June

Paid club. Eve down after tea. Letter from B/mth. Fine day. Went up to Consett in morning with chi. Expected to be fined heavily for books at library. Had them out 5 weeks studying Hitler. Only fined 5d. Librarian helped me to choose 'T.E. Lawrence by his Friends', 'Fanny by Gaslight' by Michael Sadleir. Picked 'The Valley of the Assassins' by Freya Stark myself. In garden all afternoon. Carpet of weeds. Talked with Mr. Brease ex Headmaster of C.E. School. Must be nearly 90 yrs. S.A. marched up street. Adjutant Smith shook hands with me. Love the Lord Jesus, Live well & Pray, Remarkable personality. Mrs. Gill influenced greatly by him. Sweep 6.30 Cleaned up.

Friday, 27 June

Not so warm. Cold wind. Eleanor delighted with swing on gate. Still lot to do in kitchen & scullery. Soot difficult to clean up. Felt very heavy & head achy. Probably liverish. Eleanor played with soot dumped on garden. What a sight! Shopped in afternoon. 2 eggs, 2 tins spaghetti, 4 pies, No Extras. Horrible smell of dried fish in shop. Piece of English beef. Small only 2/11. Eve down with John after tea. Sweets at McAloon's. Pictures, P O'Brien The Modern Hero. [sic – 'Knute Rockne, All American'] Story of Knute Rockne, (American) Football Coach.[7]

Saturday, 28 June

Warmer than yesterday but not brilliant. Spent morning in. Did a little washing. Only in Leadgate afternoon. Cake at McAloon's. No ice cream. Poor Bill. Got Eleanor shoes from Store. Opened tin of Strawberries for tea. Extravagance. No fresh ones to get. 3/6 per lb. No tomatoes either now they are controlled price. Must watch Harvey Lax's greenhouse. Baked white bread after tea. Bacon Pasty. Growing expert.

Sunday, 29 June

Fine day very warm afternoon. Walked Dene, White's Fields, Lower Durham Road. Carried chi blazers. Glorious flowers Fields look splendid all gold, white, purple and green. Saw first wild rose & foxglove. Long grass tickled Bill's legs.

[At top of page] Read 'T.E. Lawrence by his Friends'. Feeling of great familiarity. Was he at Westward Ho that summer in 1932? Did he give me tea at Clovelly & walk with me on the excursions? Did he ask me what I would do if I was left a fortune? Would I not like a home to come back to from my travels?

Monday, 30 June

Wire from Will. Good Day. Slow drying for washing. All ironed at night. Meeting for Committee for Jam Centre but again only 4 turned up so postponed. Not much enthusiasm. Chi left with Derrick & Mervyn but not for long. Will's wire 'fit and well'. Very thankfull [sic] after month's silence. Still in Malta.

Tuesday, 1 July

After tidying up went to Dentist's. Warm rather thundery. Cleaned & scraped teeth. Look lovely now. Agreed that Romance has no place in Dentist's Room. Pulled & twisted my mouth such shapes. No woman could look beautiful to a Dentist. Saw Bette Davis in 'All This, and Heaven Too'. 100% *art* but very sad. Had to walk home No bus such a long picture.

Wednesday, 2 July

Lovely day. In the garden again in the afternoon. Lettuce very tender but no hearts forming. Row of irises up path ruined by thunderstorm. No flowers all lying flat & broken. Sweet Williams & carnations taken root well.

Thursday, 3 July

Did bedroom & bathroom. Hoed and weeded garden. Wish I could sunburn as well as chi. They are lovely colour. Their hair is bleached lighter than ever. Told Mrs. Gill I thought I had met Lawrence. Says she "Fancy you might not have been here then but you would have been a widow", Words, spoken words, futile, silly, destructive, sullying words.

Friday, 4 July

Cleaned up kitchen Fine day. Eve down for tea. Told her I thought I had met Lawrence. She stared. Then asked if I had any decent books to lend! Went shopping with her. W.W. had no eggs left. Got 1 lb sausage, ½ lb tomatoes.

Saturday, 5 July

Fine day again. Not much to do but took time to do it. Mother got nice white pyrethrums & gypsophila for dad's grave. Afraid she talks of him to chi. Don't want them to think of him as dead & gone. She told them at tea she would not be here much longer either. Vera the Milk Girl walked into the pantry for jugs. Billy said What are you going in there for? I don't go in your pantry. Where is your pantry?

Sunday, 6 July

Very windy, Commemoration Service. Eleanor fell out of procession on seeing me. This mother complex is bad. Bill still won't go to S.School. After tea bused to Rowlands Gill walked back to Lintz Ford by the river. Saw boys bathing, shivering round fire. Had a chat with horse over wall. Bill collected mess on leg. Lucky. Had supper with me. Bed 9 pm. Very grown up. Mother at Annfield. Ella Clarke's hubby missing since April. Crete. Frank down left parcel.

[At top of page] Freya Stark, 'The Valley of the Assassins'. Rather trying to read.

Monday, 7 July

Dull day in morning but got out fine. Wished afterwards that I had washed. Did not feel too grand. Lay about all day. After going for pay walked round by Council Schools Black Lonnon & Durham Road with chi. Delighted with hedges of wild roses. Brought some home. Went to pictures.

Tuesday, 8 July

Good day. Mother went up to Consett so I had to miss appointment with Dentist. Pity. Did a little washing. Thinned out beetroot, parsnips & carrots & onions. Surprising the number of onions in a row. Hope they grow. Hoed potatoes, cabbage, leeks. Transplanted marigolds. Eve & John down for tea. I went into the garden again while they used the jam. I must be growing mean.

Wednesday, 9 July

Rather dull morning but looked promising. So after breakfast packed sandwiches and departed for Whitley with kids. First sight of sea for two years. Bill coming down street to prom "I've found the sea" Could not go on beach. But the ozone was glorious. Chi had ride in donkey cart. Bill flicked the reins with gusto. Eleanor found courage to pat baby pony. Misty afternoon. Chi had a paddle in Paddling Pool after a little hesitation. Loved ride in Electric Train. Interested in Guard. They are very good travellers. Bill intelligent observer if tiring questioner. Travelled down with couple from Villa Real who lunched at Carricks also. Chi ate adult portions 4/6. Tea in beach café. Family from Leicester opposite. In N/C for holiday. Bill caught woman's stockings with spade on bus station then mine in bus. Furious. Shame. Both of us tired. Home 8 pm. Ready for bed. Alarm 1 am–2 am(ish).

[At top of page] Gilbert Frankau – 'Self Portrait'. Self-centred, extravagant, conceited. Self-important egoist. But able to see his failings now, but sympathises with himself, I'm afraid.

Thursday, 10 July

Glorious day. Very hot. Blossoms on peas. Night scented stock looks beautiful up the path. Lupins very attractive. Bees busy. Afraid marigolds I transplanted are dead. Cleaned bedroom & bathroom. Shopped for rations. Received last week's egg rations. Long time since I had 6 eggs in a bag. First new potatoes (3d per lb). New carrots 8d a bunch. ½ lb red currants 1/-. Pies lovely this week. Must be Palethorpes. Washed chi's hair again. Mother baked. Went to pictures. Submarine Patrol. Last war. Realistic fight with sub. Eve down after tea.

Friday, 11 July

Letter from Queen. Invites Mother for visit. Glorious day. Very warm but breeze made it bearable. Cleaned up kitchen & scullery. Long rest in afternoon. Finished G. Frankau 'Self Portrait'. Extravagant conceit in youth. Went down to Butcher's. Boneless sirloin. McAloon's no cigs or sweets. Walked round Four House Fields. Corn filling out. Bill anxious about weeds. Hay cocks in fields. Prefer sound of horse reaper to motor reaper. Blossoms on Blackberries pure white. Eleanor brave in field with calves but clung to my hand. Leisha at door No word from Lawrence.

Saturday, 12 July

Wire to Will. Misty morning. Heavy atmosphere. Had headache. Expected storm, but cleared in afternoon. Went up to Consett to Library at 11 am. but found it closed. Holiday & redecoration. Sent wire to William. After dinner went to shops. Lovely ham at W.W. Fresh peas 6d per lb. McAloon's had trifle 8d. only cream worth anything. 10 Woodbines. ½ lb sweets. Mrs. Gill and sister expecting family from Glasgow. Lazy night knitting, reading, listening in.

Sunday, 13 July

Misty, rather cold. Chi played with next door chi. Six extra. (4 chi) 3 Gill boys sleep at Pickerings. Treaty of Alliance with USSR broadcast at 2 pm. Raids on Malta Friday & Sat. New potatoes, green peas mint sauce sirloin for dinner. Lovely. Hilda Meek & Mrs. Kay visited after tea. Never seen her since my early teens. Still has adenoids & rather deaf, but very different woman from the girl we avoided. Frank down.

[At top of page] T.E. Lawrence, 'Revolt in the Desert' overshadowed this week completely.

Monday, 14 July

Washing Day, Big wash. Done fairly early.

Tuesday, 15 July

Wire from William. All well. Posted letter to B/mth (10/-) Also card to Will.

Wednesday, 16 July

Cleaned bedrooms.

Thursday, 17 July

Fine Day. District W.I. Meeting for Programme Planning. Well attended. I did not know other Leadgate members till afternoon when Mrs. Forster & Mrs H. Turnbull arrived. Demonstration of debate. I spoke for our group against officers should voluntarily resign after 3 yrs. Dreadful empty feeling when looking down at faces but won 50–50 vote. Women in front put me off grand finale. With prepared speech feel sure I could make a show. Sez me. Two years today I sailed away from my husband & Malta.

Friday, 18 July

Letter from Will written July 4th. Lovely. Says he has garden & hens. Family man. Quiet time. Also letter from B/mth with

Insurance Card. Only 18/1 for two quarters & I always sent at least £1 for one quarter!! And a surplus benefit is paid every New Year! Pleasant surprise after paying six years.

Sunday, 20 July

Fine day. After dinner went down to Scotswood to see Auntie Nellie. Chi rather bored. Nothing for them to do but enjoyed ride down Low Road by River Derwent.

[At top of page] 'Seven Pillars of Wisdom'. Wonderful deep understanding of Man. Minute detail of scenery in spite of active mental strain. "The poor little man."

Monday, 21 July

Posted Will's Insurance. Fine day. Washed chi clothes. No bedding & towels. Ironed. Cleaned up. Easy day. Institute Meeting. Fine Lecture on Soap by Lady Lecturer from Pelaw C.W.S.[8] "Now ladies". Too meaty. No sweet airy trifles. My pullover won 1st Place for pulled out wool re-knitted

Tuesday, 22 July

Glorious day. Cleaned up. Prepared dinner. Down to Jam Centre. Home 5.30 pm.

[Following entry written in Monday's] Jam Centre in afternoon. No table, No chairs. Back nearly broken picking up rhubarb off floor, cutting it up onto papers. Prepared fruit. Squeezed & grated lemons.

[Back to Tuesday] Deserve medal. Very tired. Trouble over weighing sugar. Mrs. Dixon weighed it again after Mrs. H.T. Turnbull found 10 lbs were 10 ozs short. Made great song about it. I suggested Mrs. H.T. had been too careful. Mrs. D. too generous. Passed over. Grumbles at no table. Grate too fine or too big. All Mrs. H.T. fault as secretary. Poor woman. Nobody ever helps her.

Wednesday, 23 July

Fine day. Eve down early to butcher's. Eleanor went back with her. After dinner I went to Jam Centre. Asked Mother to take Bill & collect Eleanor. Made 3 lbs of jam. Very proud, very tired at 7 pm. Mother returned with Eleanor 7.45 pm. No Bill. He had walked on in front of them. Wouldn't return. Never seen again. What a night I had. Went to Consett. Caught Eve getting on bus for Leadgate. No News. Asked Policeman on Market. Reported case. Walked to Crookhall in case he tried down there. Back up Fell Path. No signs. Back to Delves. Ralph went out to seek him up back streets. Mother arrived at 9.30 pm. to say he had walked in & broken down utterly exhausted. Walked home from Knitsley. True story as pieced together later. Walked to Knitsley Farm for Milk. On way back Bill wanted coat off. Eve insisted on keeping it on. Bill walked off. Wouldn't turn down street to Eve's. Went on. Mother & Eve thought he would return. They went home for Eleanor's coat. How long they stayed? Followed up on bus. Never saw him. I must have passed him also to bus. Poor lad. But he knew his way home.

Thursday, 24 July

Receipt for Will's insurance received. After last night's excitement & the day's work felt very tired all day. Reaction. Bill very subdued. But insists he was Not lost. Knew his way home. Will not do it again. Down to Jam Centre for an hour tying up jars & labelling with Mrs. Turnbull. Mrs. Dixon arrived when nearly finished. Went to pictures at night. Bill indulged in a little bloodletting while I was out. Bed in fearful state. Is this his reaction?

Friday, 25 July

Mother very busy with herself cleaning up for Ella's arrival. Also baking. I couldn't be left to do that on such an important occasion. Scullery not done till tea time as baking going on nearly all day. Blackberry test (¾ lb) Washing day. Sheets pillow cases off bed. Trimmed hedges. Weeded. Garden looks well. Peas podded.

Saturday, 26 July

Fine day. Mother off early to meet Ella in Town. After cleaning up & tidying everywhere chi & I went up to Consett. Did a little shopping. Found Mother & E. home when we arrived. Very tired. Come straight off night shift. Frank down, she in bed but soon got up. Eve down also. Put chi to bed & went to pictures. Not bad. Ella brought Eleanor pr of sox. Bill toy car & pr of pyjamas.

Sunday, 27 July

Lovely day. Ella enjoyed dinner. Chi still on best behaviour. Bill on look out for 'little bird' that carries the news to Bolton. Ella & Frank went up to Eve's for supper. Mrs. Wright down for tea. Little gentle looking old lady with silvery hair & man's deep voice. E Boat raid on Valletta harbour. Also air raid on Sat.

Monday, 28 July

Lovely day. Washed and ironed. Took all day over it. Sun nearly overpowered me when hanging clothes out. Ella & Frank hiked to Muggleswick with their teas. Goal was Edmondbyers but rain put them off. Went down for pay. Then up to Consett Library. (Let's face the Facts) Sent EFM [Expeditionary Force Message] Wire to Will 2/6 for 3 phrases chosen from list. Just give numbers & address.

Tuesday, 29 July

Fine day. Rain in afternoon. Cleared up later. Ella & Frank at Coombe Bridges. Frank arrived with new bag. Easy day. Knitted & read. Pictures at night. Tragedy, sob stuff. Council now tarred roads all round. Bill explained simply to me how it's done. &

not so simply how he was covered with tar. He followed them round all day. Began Eleanor's jersey. Green. Fairisle band brown, yellow, red.

Wednesday, 30 July

Fine day. Mother, Ella & Eleanor visited Durham in morning. Bill decided against going. Eleanor no desire to stay with me but promised to come back. Had grand time evidently. She was very grown up when she returned. Went down to Jam Centre helped Mrs. Forster to make 8 lbs jam. Mrs. Topin (has the merriest happiest blue eyes I've seen) & Mrs. Chatt (rather a sour face) made 7 lbs. Labelled, tied up end cut papers of all the jam there. Ella & Frank out somewhere for tea. Cleaned bedrooms.

Thursday, 31 July

Not too promising. Wet & misty afternoon & evening. Ella & Frank at Newcastle & Whitley Bay. Soaked. Glad to come home. Ella acquired new hat (boater) Frank afraid to go in to choose it in case she walked out without one. Cleaned pantry & china cupboard. Shopped for rations in afternoon. Asked W. Wilson if they would buy Institute Jam. Agreed. Offered 3½ lbs red currants. Went up to Council Offices to find price. Uncontrolled. Mrs. Ogle brought them up at 10 pm. Too late to do anything. Frank left early as he felt ill. Cold, shivery headache.

Friday, 1 August

B/mth 10/-. Summer is flying. Dark nights with us once more. Cleaned up downstairs windows, cement paths polishing etc. Went shopping. Took red currants to Mrs. Turnbull. 1/- per lb. Went down at 5.15 pm. to help make jam with Mrs. Forster. Never started till 7 pm. Gassing & Mrs. Turnbull arrived. Did not look too pleased but did help. Jam finished 9.30 pm. Lovely. Red C. & rhubarb. Ella had supper ready. Frank down. All signs of flu gone. Posted letter to B/mth. 10/-.

Saturday, 2 August

Fine day. Finished early. Ella left for 9.55 am. bus Leaves N/C Central 12 noon. Mother depressed. Eleanor wanted to go with her. Bill says he could walk home when he wanted to see me. Up street before dinner. Still no eggs. Mr. Lax brought tomatoes for Ella too late. Did some weeding in afternoon. Hoed up cabbages, etc. No cake at McAloon's No Sweets No Ices No Cigs. Luxuries easily done without. Mother returned 9.30 pm. Life Certificate asked for again. Must never have received it fortnight ago. Mrs. Pickering signed it.

Sunday, 3 August

Wire from Will. Fit & well. Exactly same as last. Glorious day. Pleasant breeze. Raspberry tart for tea. Bus ride to Ebchester with Mother after tea. River looked very inviting. Bill asked, Will it be there tomorrow? Crowds down. Crossed old bridge. Saw garden with fat onions, big cauliflower peas sweet peas. Bill. Where does the river go? Later. What makes the lights light?

Monday. 4 August

Dull wet & miserable day. Chi inside all afternoon. Not a bit holiday-ish. Finished Seven Pillars of Wisdom. Will throw off his spell now.

[In pencil] Walk after tea with Bill. Young colt tried to edge us off path into field.

[In ink again] Cut brown linen frock down to overall to wear with blouse. Washed two frocks for Mother & ironed them. Mrs. Pickering gave birth to daughter at 4.30 am.

Tuesday, 5 August

Heavy showers all day. Windy. Bill's delight to take Snip for a walk. Other boys very pally with him then. Mother up at Eve's for lunch. Baked bread & oatmeal biscuits. Two biscuits left after tea. Eve & John for tea. Jam Centre 5 pm. Labelled covered &

tied. Mrs. M. Turnbull scrubbed out. Went back 7.15 pm. to check wt. 80 lbs. Some leftovers missing! Display by 2 aeroplanes. Whistled over roof tops. Pictures. Maryland. Coloured. horses. hunt. 11 pm. Siren. All clear 11.45 pm. Nothing to hear.

Wednesday, 6 August

Cloudy morning but cleared out later. After dinner took chi down to Shotley Bridge Spa grounds (Mrs. Dinning) Trees in plenty to run round. Garden enormous. Rasps in plenty but all ordered. 6d paid for 2 cabbages & 1 lb beetroot. 6d bunch of flowers, mass of sweet peas and spirea. Delightful; colours. Home 8.30 pm. Little Dorothy wanted to give Eleanor 2 of her old frocks. Couldn't refuse. Slept soundly.

[In pencil] Third anniversary of Dad's death. Pea pods filling. Mother, Eleanor & Bill go out every morning to have a pea. Eleanor constantly among the peas. We will never have a boiling.

Thursday, 7 August

Washed chi clothes, undies, cottons. Cleaned scullery. Afterwards Mrs. Gill took Eleanor to see Baby Pickering. Remembered in time to give her piece of silver to present to baby for luck. Caught Mrs. G. looking through her purse as if to give Eleanor's silver herself. Old Spanish Custom. Eleanor & Bill rather washed out today. Put to bed with aspirin. Looks like a cold coming. Went to pictures. Feel like a good drink. Wish I dare.

[In pencil] Shopped in afternoon but forgot to take Ration Card.

Friday, 8 August

Paid club up to date.

[In pencil] Eleanor has a fearful cold. Nearly sneezed her head off. Eyes swollen. Bill O.K. Cleaned kitchen Ironed clothes

Cleaned bedroom Mother did bathroom & stairs. Shopped in afternoon. ¾lb currants. Asked for Eve's eggs but she had got them. Finished Fairisle Pattern on Eleanor's Jersey. Some wind & rain. Not very warm. Mother out at night.

Saturday, 9 August

[In pencil] Not bad day till evening then rained heavily. Took flowers up to churchyard with chi. After tea went down to McAloon's for cake & cigs. Got 60 fags but no cake. So baked red currant tart. Currant square coconut buns & chocolate cake. Not bad. Mother out all day before dinner till 8.45 pm.

[In ink] Brought 3 lbs gooseberries home.

Sunday, 10 August

Very windy day but fine. Mother made gooseberry jam after dinner. 5 lbs jam. Lovely. Eleanor went to S. School. Bill stayed at home and picked the peas. Saw Mrs. Pickering & baby. Lovely girl Mavis. Bill wants brother to play with but Eleanor must have sister in case she wants to play with his brother, I guess. Listened to Queen's broadcast. Lovely voice.

[At top of page] 'Memory Hold-the-Door' John Buchan. Very proper and right. Thoroughly Presbyterian. But interesting descriptions of people & places. The Borders, South Africa. T.E. Lawrence.

Monday, 11 August

Letter from B/mth. Wash day. Not very promising at first but fine windy day by dinner time. All dried by tea time then rain fell heavily. P.O. for pay. Consett P.O. to send wire to William. Also Library. Miss Craig asked Mother to tell me to attend meeting of Ladies Working Party at 6.30 pm. Gala Day Aug 23rd discussed. Later called for key to Jam Centre but son (Willie) couldn't find it. So walked to Iveston & back with Snip.

Tuesday, 12 August

Fine but windy, Cleaned up then ironed clothes. Went down to Jam Centre for hour. Labelled, covered & finished of jars of jam. Very damp. Mrs. H. Turnbull told of disappearance of leftovers. Eve down after tea. Wrote to Barrisford for Mother to say she would arrive Thursday. Mother went off to Medomsley Edge. One cluster of red roses on climbing plant out. Very very late in blooming.

Wednesday, 13 August

Showery in morning. Fair afternoon Wet evening. Cleaned kitchen. Washed out bedroom. Chi upstairs with me all time. Eleanor brought all the dusters she could find and they both polished two old suitcases. Had some of MY OWN carrots boiled for dinner. Lovely. Went for walk after tea over Four House Fields. Too late to watch Milking. Bill disappointed. Heavy rain fell minute after we got home. Mother went over to Hannah Lax's for whist drive. Alarm at dinner time. Mother heard Tynemouth & Jarrow were bombed & machine gunned. Mother packed bag today. Excited over holiday.

Thursday, 14 August

Fine, sunny but windy. Mother up early. Cleaned her bedroom after breakfast. Anxious to get away. Left at 2 pm. after keeping chi 'het up' about rabbits, cows & fields all morning. Important announcement at 3 pm by Attlee, Privy Seal, [9] that Roosevelt & Churchill met in mid-ocean & declared Peace Aims. [10] Who has Control of the High Seas? Two alarms through night. Three 'enemy overhead' alarms at Works. Heard plane circle round but nothing else.

Friday, 15 August

Fine day. Rained in evening. Cleaned kitchen & scullery. Shopped in afternoon. Chi stayed home with Mervyn & Derrick.

No eggs or jam. Pressed beef, also tin of fruit. Mrs. H. Turnbull up street said Eve had carried eggs for me to Jam Centre three times and I'm not there to get them. What a blow! I never expected such a favour. Margie put chi to bed & stayed in. Ladies Working Party Meeting. Put on Refreshment Committee for Dance & Gala. Busy Public Life. Went to pictures later. Alarm at 10 pm. Left cinema in case Margie was alarmed. But she was O.K.

Saturday, 16 August
Bright morning, windy cold afternoon & evening. Tidied round. Up to Library before 12. No time to choose book. Lunched at Hanson's Café. Bill & Eleanor thrilled & so grown up. Then matinee, 'Flight Command' good. Robt. Taylor handsome, Ruth Hussey wonderful study of glamorous wife. Bought 2 lbs bath salts at Wworths. Smells! Alarm through the night again. Letter from Mother to Bill. Arrived safely. Making raspberry cake & rasp jam.

Sunday, 17 August
Showery, colder windy. Pulled my own peas, carrots parsnips for dinner. Wish I'd tried potatoes. Steak & Kidney Pie. Baked apples. Lazy day. Read silly novel (W. Deeping! Such a comedown) Listened to Gracie Fields. Something gone from her attraction. Is it just the fact she sailed away & left us? But she has come back & is doing service.

[At top of page] 'John Brown Autobiography.' S. Shields boy struggle to find work finally admitted to Ruskin College. Socialist.

Monday, 18 August
Letter to B/mth 10/-. Washed chi clothes, undies, socks. Fine day. Visited P.O. for pay Received new book. Went up to Consett Library. Two fiction books. Women's Institute Meeting 6.30 pm. Eleanor in bed beforehand. Bill stayed with Gill's boys.

Talk on Gas very clear & helpful. Decided on Produce Show next month. Asked me to talk on Malta. Invitation to meeting to discuss Future Educational Moves nearly thrown out. Thought to be Political. 'One of them Communistic things'. Offered to pay own expenses. Accepted. Bill tired but very keen to have supper with me. "*P*[?] to Meeting. Where's the meat? Did you not bring any home?" Siren through the night.

Tuesday, 19 August

Not so bad, windy & showery. Ironed washing. Lazy. "dreaming idle dreams" of what might have been. Miss Craig brought 50 programmes for Sat. sports and book of raffle tickets. Don't know where I'll sell them. Mrs. Telford sent Margaret Tinley all round this area. Works Danger Overhead signal went twice through night. Heard plane but nothing else.

Wednesday, 20 August

Showery but fine intervals. Took up three heads of potatoes. Good but will have to be used soon as show signs of scabs. Carrots parsnips & peas again used for dinner. Nothing better than vegs. straight out of garden. Mrs. Lax in for over an hour. Eve down with John after tea. Wanted to go to lav. or would not have called. John delighted in taking Raffle Tickets round. Betty Breen later took them out & brought 4/6 back. Mother returned 8 pm. complete with two rabbits, apples raspberry jam (not boiled – real flavour) bottled rasps. Eggs.

[At top of page] 'War by Revolution' – Francis Williams. Clear simple style. Understandable contrary to most Political books. Only way to destroy Nazism is by Revolutionary Democracy. Win people [On next page] with New Order of Democracy. New Ideal that will defeat Nazi ideal.

Thursday, 21 August

Fine day. Spent a little time in garden hoeing and weeding. Rain brought fine crop of weeds. Chi played houses all day. Bill in his tent, Eleanor on her mat. Mother baked. Rabbit pie for dinner. Consett Library again. W Wilson for rations. No eggs. ½lb raisins, bottle of sauce, Y. Relish. Meeting 7 pm. for Refreshments Committee. Dance off. Adjutant declares hall full of undeclared goods. Cannot be cleared. Pictures. Wm. Boyd as Hopalong Cassidy. Very dark on coming out.

Friday, 22 August

Cleaned kitchen scullery. Fine day. Mother at Eve's most of the day. Must remember Club. Shopped after tea for Meat. Bought marrow. Eve & John down. John took Raffle tickets round again. One woman wanted 2d change. Then John says I had an idea. I went back and told her to buy another ticket then she wouldn't want any change. She did. Took Bill & Eleanor to pictures to see 'Texas Rangers Ride Again'.

Saturday, 23 August

Doubtful morning but cleared to glorious day. Gala Day. Made sandwiches 11 am to 12.45 pm. Washed & dressed nibs then went back to Refreshment Room at Welfare Ground 2 pm. to 7.30 pm. Never off my feet. How tired. First sitting down (Colonel Wereker etc.) second H[ome] G[uard] officers complained of tea. Tasted of paraffin chloride of lime?? etc. Grand spread. Even to Fruit loaf with almond icing. Homes Boys Band for tea. Thought they would never stop. Amount made not reckoned up yet. Mrs. Dunning told my fortune. Jealousy all round me. As one door shuts, another opens.

Sunday, 24 August

Glorious day but very lazy. Washed my hair & had bath in afternoon. Only as far as garden to pick peas carrots potatoes for dinner.

[At top of page]: 'Dare to live' – I. Hurst. Left typewriter to tramp & hitch hike all over world. 'Testament of Joad' – C.M. Joad. Meaning of life lies in sane & healthy enjoyment of same. (Lin Yutang 'My Country & My Life' [sic – 'My Country and My People'])

Monday, 25 August

Showery day but lovely evening. Weather put me off washing but too wet to take a trip. Bill disappeared to neighbours reappeared at intervals with demands for canes paper string glue, finally appeared with a kite. Collected allowance from P.O. Changed books at Library. Saunter round Consett shops. One or two lovely satin blouses lovely price also. Home. Miss Craig had called taken Programme money. Meeting for tomorrow. 7 pm. Mother couldn't say where. Put chi to bed by 7.15 pm. Went to pictures as Mother was matting.

Tuesday, 26 August

British forces enter Iran in S. Russian forces in N. Cloudy outlook at first, few spots of rain but wind drove clouds away. Washed & finished by 2.15 pm. Dried lovely. Had to watch chi as Clifford P[ears] has whooping cough & will not keep away. Chi started school today so Bill rather lonesome. Sent Will Birthday Greetings by E.F.M. Tried all shops for cigs. Woodbines are killing me. No luck. Bought ¼lb mushrooms for 6d. ¼lb blackberries 7½d, W.W. for bacon. Lucky to visit they had eggs got 3. Meeting Mrs. Turnbull's Turned in 11/6 Raffle money. Man waiting for bus asked to draw winning ticket. Amount raised for Gala £35 so far received.

Wednesday, 27 August

Wet windy cold. Chi at odds with themselves. In and out all day. Blackberry sponge pudding with custard for dinner. Lovely. Too small. Cleaned bedroom & bathroom. Went up later &

found poe spilt and bath salts all over floor & bath dirty. Chi's work. Each blamed the other. Ironed all afternoon. Tired & nervy tonight. Posted MSS. Such hopes. Such ambition.

Thursday, 28 August

Fine day. Took chi into N/castle for day. Soon tired of shops. Lunch at Bainbridge's 4/6. (Soup fish & potatoes). Tea at Carricks. Heaps of jam & milk Bread cakes ice-cream 2/11. Bought Camel Hair Wool for socks but could not bring it with me as coupons not in Ration Book. Went to News Theatre. Eleanor slept. Bill very interested. Film on Kentucky horses. Straight to bed.

Friday, 29 August

William's birthday* Fine day. Hope Will had peaceful birthday. Ella wrote of friend Helen. May come here for few days to be near boy soldier. Get in Rations. No eggs. Only Woodbines.

Saturday, 30 August

Fine day. Posted Ella's letter with P.O. for 13/10 to pay for Bill's pyjamas.

Sunday, 31 August

Lovely day. Chi at Sunday School. Bill not at all keen. Walk after tea down lane. Frank called 2 pm. Mother at Eve's.

[At top of page] The New Order by C.P. Purdam. Security for all. Education – only the best will be available for all Health State Doctors Hospitals.

Monday, 1 September

Damp heavy morning, but sunny afternoon. Washed. Collected pay in afternoon. Owed Mrs. Pinkerton (Stamp Lady) for 4 savings stamps, took it up. Asked me in. Really nice room Not like Park Villas a bit. Whitish paper, Horizontal lines. Fireplace not black but enamelled fawns brown (mottled) heavy mantelpiece, Low sideboard & polished gate leg table. Fawn carpet. Not at all Working Class taste. Husband barber. Alarm 10 pm–12 pm. Plane overhead. Got chi up. Bombs dropped Bladen Jesmond Shieldfield Walker. Bad night.

Tuesday, 2 September

Fine hot day again. Ironed washing before dinner. Spent some time in garden. Bill tried to catch butterfly Red Indian style: on hands & knees. Demanded silence. Missed brown butterflies this year. Eleanor & Mira in garden eating tops of onions. Bill reset the night-scented stock I pulled out of border. Went to pictures at night.

Wednesday, 3 September

Another lovely day. Cleaned bedroom & downstairs Weeded part of garden. Mrs. Gill came in early to tell us Capt. Warner had died in Infirmary overnight. News only known when John Collinson rang up in morning to ask how he was. Rang District Commissioner to break news to Mrs. Warner. Mira (Capt. Daughter) played here with chi all day. Had meals here as well though officially at Mrs Gill's. Mira here. Mrs. Warner visited husband. Not appendicitis. Ruptured *spleen* but something else pending. Seriously ill. In great pain. Siren Mrs. Warner alone with Mira (Mrs. Gill would not let Margy go down) John Collinson went for them during alarm. Took them to his home. So they missed policeman who went to call Mrs. Warner to Infirmary where Capt. was dying. This fact not told to Mrs. Warner on Thurs.

Thursday, 4 September

Brother George's birthday. 30 yrs old! Glorious Day. Felt very restless. Went for rations. No sugar as consignment burnt in Mon. raid on N/castle. Expected later. No eggs. ½lb dates. After dinner went into Town. Called for Camel Hair Wool held back for me. Prices terrific. 4½ gns tricycle too small for Bill.

Watering can (toy) 1/-½ Tiny doll 7½d Honey for tea. Assistant at Lily's shop related horrors of Mon. raid. Street top & bottom of her house bombed Shrieks & cries of women & chi. Small boy scratched himself out of debris in white pyjamas. Get my nanny out. Machine gunned street. AFS men.[11] No water, no gas, no trains or buses to work.

Friday, 5 September

Fine day. Cleaned kitchen scullery etc. Washed all lace curtains, creamed them. Look pretty. Not out. Mother off somewhere. Let Derrick & Mervyn take envelopes out for Sailors' Fund. (3d each) Marion Hall round with raffle tickets. Money for W. Working Party Funds. Parcel of soap, soap powder, etc. Collected 25/9. Eve down. Sold table cloth for 3 weeks club money. Parcel from Ella. Hankies for Eleanor. Candy cigs for John & Bill, Sweets for Mother. Letter for me. No mention of P.O. I sent.

Saturday, 6 September

Glorious morning. Cool & damp afternoon & evening but no rain. Cleared up. Went to Library Consett for fresh books. After dinner collected envelopes for Sailors' Fund. Took over 2 hrs. So much gossiping. Collected £1-15-1. Very good for small district and poorly paid at that. Sugar not arrived. Six small cakes. But 9 eggs! Mother at Mrs. Humes funeral. Not out in evening. Very tired.

Sunday, 7 September

Fine day. Eleanor has touch of diarrhoea. Day of National Prayer. Short walk over Four House Fields. Corn sheaves stooked (?). Bill wanted to know exact process of mills to make flour. 6 pm. & 9 pm. News announce Soviet War Meeting. Call for Unity of Women against Hitler. Have written scathing letter to BBC. Still considering my MSS which demands same. Siren 10–10.30 pm. Finished green jersey for Eleanor.

[At top of page] 'The Astonishing Island' – W. Holtby. England as seen by simple foreigner. Brilliant satire.

Monday, 8 September

Not so fine. Dampish. A little rain in afternoon. Tidied house. Eleanor better. Bill still playing tents. Alan [Agar] off school because Sailor Dad home on leave. Bill wonders how he gets on & off ships. Heard him tell Mrs. Gill he had a 'ghost'. Does it bite? No. Where is it? Here. What do you want it for? Well to milk what do you think? Collected pay. Posted indignant letter to BBC. Registered for Onions but scolded for being late. Received last week's sugar ration. Started socks for Bill. Mended Eleanor's & Bill's trousers.

Thursday, 11 September

Wire from Will at 6.30 pm. Well & fit. What a relief after 6 weeks silence.

Friday, 12 September

Christmas parcels for Middle East to be posted by Sept. 18th.

Saturday, 13 September

Very cloudy morning. But warm afternoon in Town 'Conference on New Educational Order'. Speeches by Dr. Stead (Chief Educ. Officer of Chesterfield) & Mr. Greene (Gen. Sec. for W.E.A.) Wild political remarks by delegates when meeting thrown open for discussion. My speech listened to Chairman gave me extra ½ mins. No more favours. Walked on air till I thought of all I should have said.

Sunday, 14 September

Nice day. Baked Christmas cake for Will. Looks lovely.

Monday, 15 September

Not bad day. Tidied house. Collected allowance. Changed books at library. Cobblers for shoes. Women's Institute Meeting 6.30 pm. Garden Produce Show. Marvellous onions & leeks. Gave talk on Life in Malta. Interested meeting. Members also gave me a clap for speaking at Newcastle but no opportunity to read notes on Conference. Mrs. Wilson proud to tell of her husband in charge of Stores on Expedition to Spitzbergen and Archangel Russia. Home safe.

Wednesday, 17 September

Letters from Will & Chan. Well & fit. Chan sounds bright & cheerful. Got his third stripe. Will wistful.

Thursday, 18 September

Spent all morning packing Will's parcel. Cake, jar of gooseberry jam, 2 prs. socks, aspirin, laxatives, Beecham's Powders, foot powder, 2 cakes soap, Shaving soap, box of brilliantine, one hanky, 2 oz. of Three Nuns tobacco, few chocolates, 2 Mittens, 2 magazines. Sewed tin box in old tablecloth. Eve did not arrive as promised with anything to pack. Cost 2/- to post. Sent hankies & letter to Chan.

Friday, 19 September

Posted Xmas cards to Will & Chan. Meeting of Refreshment Committee. Ada Walton filled the room. Went home later with her to help prepare vegetables given from gardens to make Salads to sell at ARP Sports. Can't get my hands clean now.

Saturday, 20 September

Posted Calendar to Will. A.R.P. Sports Day. Fettled teas all afternoon till after 6 pm. Bill stayed round Pavilion & had a couple of sandwiches. Disappeared with penny for ice-cream. Eleanor never came near. Ada's salads were very good.

Sunday, 21 September

Quiet day. Walked down Dene & over fields to Iveston. Picked a few ripe blackberries. Chi collected straw & brought it home to play with.

[At top of page] 'Freedom in the Modern World' – John MacMurray. Need for emotional revival of faith. Only real persons in real contact with real life can be free. Real contact means real friendships.

Monday, 22 September

Washed chi's clothes. Dried slowly. Collected allowance. Posted letter to B/mth (10/-) Letters to Ella & Joan. Card to Will.

Tuesday,23 September

Not bad day. Wind from South so clothes dried slowly. Washed 2 blankets, shawl flannel sheets.

Wednesday, 24 September

Damp morning Chi stayed in writing, cutting up papers for bacon rashers. Bill had omelette pan on, hot Nearly burnt it. Went Cinema Matinee. Saw 'Target for Tonight'. Eleanor slept. Bill interested.

[At top of page] 'This is our World' – Kurt Lubinski. Travels in Abyssinia, Iceland, Siberia, U.S.A., N. Africa, Spain.

Thursday, 25 September

Misty haze over everything. Cleaned scullery & pantry as well as kitchen today. Bill asked if fishes do poo poos. If so what colour do they make the water? Mother stuck into her mat so I went to the pictures. Felt as if my spirits needed raising.

Friday, 26 September

Not bad day. Cleaned kitchen. In afternoon went for Rations. Made bill up to 15/6 and so got 1lb mixed Dried Fruits. No eggs this week. Chose joint off leg of mutton. Harry let me have 5

Players, 5 Darts [brands of cigarette]. Mother finished fireside mat and chi revelled in it, rolled about like kittens. Bill quite proud of it. Mrs. Coulson taken ill. Poisoned stomach. Taken to Newcastle Infirmary.

Saturday, 27 September

Misty moisty morning. Windy. Changed Eleanor into woollies & Bill wore pullover. But fine afternoon. Walked in Consett Park and felt very hot. Daddy would love to see the stretches of green grass. Leaves changing colour, many fallen. Consett streets crowded. Got Bill pair of braces. Have been scarce. Rainy evening. Queue for Roxy down to the bridge. Got to the steps but did not wait for chance of seat. Heard [Jacqueline] Dalya,[12] voice in a 1000. Glorious deep powerful. Mrs. Coulson died about 2 pm. Shock for everybody.

Sunday, 28 September

Fine day but damp. Rain overnight. Mignonette smells sweet. Frank & Maggie here after tea. Maggie full of talk of daughter Lilian's wedding. She's got everything but is waiting for a house. Rainy evening. Works hooter blew twice about 10.40 pm. No sound.

Monday, 29 September

Fine bracing day, keen wind bright sun. Cold starry moonlight night. Searchlights insignificant beside Her Majesty. Cleaned up kitchen & washed. Partly ironed before dark. Mother on the trail of a kettle, the aluminium one developed a leak last night. Bought another certificate today (N). Sent off P.O. to Insurance and Book Club. Free from debt except for Dentist. Went to pictures. Bill wore new shirt. Looks so grown up.

Tuesday, 30 September

Wire from Will. Fit and well. Fine day. Finished ironing. Over to Medomsley Edge Busty Pit for conference to plan next year's

W.I. meetings. Miss Hall very nice. Blackberry Week starts Oct. 10th. So Bill starts school with week's holiday. Mrs. Turnbull gave me two Bantam eggs for chi. Walked home. Enjoyed quick walk with no chi to slow me down.

Wednesday, 1 October
Not bad day again but dampish. Mrs. Coulson buried Today. Mother upset. Cleaned bedrooms etc.

[At top of page] Faked Passport[s] – Dennis Wheatley. Good spy story of early part of this war. Finnish War with Russia. Goering clever able statesman.

Thursday, 2 October
Fine day. Did scullery etc. Took Chi down to Aunt Maggie's Annfield. Mother went to N/C and Scotswood. Walk round Annfield shops for sweets. ¼lb lucky. Swing in Park. Siren went at 8 pm. Caught 8.30 bus home. All clear about 11 pm. Bad night for N. Shields etc. Letters to Ella returned. No such address.

Friday, 3 October
Not bad day. Dampish. Eve down after dinner. Had to ask her for cig. Shopping afterwards. No eggs again. ½lb raisins tin of milk. Jam for month. Bill put halfpennies in Stamp Machine for stamps to write to Daddy. Letter from U.S.A. and from B/mth.

Saturday, 4 October
Fine day. Chi playing schools in garden all afternoon. Hardly time for tea. Loved it. Bill knew his numbers up to 10. Eleanor eager to learn. Got ¼lb toffees, ¼lb slab of Rowntree's Choc. 2 *Bigg* bars of choc. ¼lb choc. Round the shops. Pictures at night.

Sunday, 5 October
Misty moisty rainy day. Eleanor's cough a little better. Frank down. Just escaped a large piece of shrapnel on Thurs. night. Man's sleeve cut by piece. Wrote to Mrs. Chas. Hoferbier Portsmouth Iowa. Card to Will.

[At top of page] 'The Story of San Michele' – Axel Munthe. Life as doctor among epidemics earthquakes, the idle rich, the diseased poor.

Monday, 6 October

Misty moisty morning. Ground very wet. Really played around tidying up. P.O. for allowance. Posted American letter and Will's card. Too many people in to ask Mrs. P. to sign Declaration sent by Paymaster. Made a round of the shops, (1) ¼ lb boiled sweets + 20 Du Maurier Cigs (2) 20 Players Weights & 10 Woodbines (3) 5 Woodbines & 1d P.K. Mrs. McAloon signed Declaration. Carried it up street Gave it to Ivor to post. Remembered in pictures I'd never signed it. Margaret Crosby went into Murray's H. to have tonsils removed. David C. burnt his hand on fireplace.

Tuesday, 7 October

Another damp morning so did not wash but later washed chi's things. Brightened out after dinner. Chi and I went to look for blackberries with Eleanor's little basket and paper bag. Down Dene to Black's first field. Went down hedge first near path. Bill found plenty 'catarrhs' (haws) Eleanor picked green berries. But on wrong side of hedge. Sunny side at the other side. Found hole in hedge crawled through. Found plenty. Bill good picker. Filled basket. Thresher at White's Farm. Ready for late tea. Mrs. Crosby in to say goodbye. Off to Haltwhistle again. Upset by David's accident. Finished rough writing of Memories.

Wednesday, 8 October

Damp again but not cold. Bright afternoon quite warm. Margaret Crosby brought home. OK. Mrs. Crosby departed. Letter from Ella advising Mother not to visit her just yet. Mother very disappointed. Took Eleanor to Shotley Bridge this afternoon. E. very bucked. Bill played at selling kippers up the street. I wasted afternoon in daydreams. Must put them behind me. Face realities. MSS returned again. Blackberry pudding for dinner not big enough.

Thursday, 9 October

Busy cleaning bedrooms etc. Wire from daddy to Son William greeting his birthday. Bill showed it to all.

Friday, 10 October

Bill 5 yrs old Today. A Man. Such excitement. Six birthday cards. Parcel (Book) from Auntie Ella. Prayer Book from Cousin John, 2 Drawing Books pencil & chalks from Gill's boys. Plasticine from Mrs. Crosby, It seems incredible, 5 yrs since I felt him kick my legs when he was delivered. 5 yrs since Uncle Frank cried "he's got golden lashes," 5 yrs since I cried because his father was not there to see him and he is not here again. Gill's boys & Cousin John were here to tea. Very small Birthday Cake. I forgot to put ½ doz. éclairs on the Table. Happy Day – only one shadow, no Daddy. Mervyn Gill's birthday also, 11 yrs old.

Saturday, 11 October

Garden white with frost, but sun chased it away. Fine day but chill wind. Not much to do. Consett in afternoon. Library, Cobblers. 3 eggs at W. Wilson's. 1lb Blackberries 5½d easier than picking them but not better. Enjoy the sun. Went into Gill's for tea. Manoeuvres on. ARP, Home Guard, etc, on duty all day. During Sun. night Leadgate & Consett taken by 'Invaders'.

Sunday, 12 October

Fine day. Bill's new Prayer Book did not 'tice him to S. School but he went. Eleanor took old P[rayer] Book & Gas Mask. Mother went up to Eve's after tea. We had quiet walk round fields. Mother fell at bus stand, hurt her knee. Alarm 11 pm-ish–12.40. Heard Jerries' planes. Saw member of W.I. on walk. Reminded her of Meeting on Wed. said, yes she would come to give me vote on Committee. No such thought in my mind.

Monday, 13 October

Bright morning changed to rain (heavy) after tea. Washed. Not quite dried but enough for ironing. Pictures at night. P.O. for allowance. Called at Squeaker Turnbull's shop. Mrs. T. said a Member had told her I was to be nominated for President of W.I. What ambition. 'Invaders' dominate village. Constant streams of tanks etc. Bill down at corner all day. Gun mounted at corner. We are in the hands of the enemy. Book & Birthday Card from George & Queen.

Tuesday, 14 October

Dull day, showery, brief sunny spells. High wind afternoon. Ironed washing. Mother baked. Eleanor proud to go down to Ross' for yeast. Bill played with Gill's boys all day. Eve & John down for short while.

Wednesday, 15 October

Fine but windy. Mother posted Ella's winter boots then took chi. to pictures after tea. W.I. Meeting 2.30 pm. Rather small meeting but better than before. Nominations for 12 Committee members made. My name down. Passed that I should be delegate to The Autumn Council Meeting, Bishop Auckland. Others afraid of writing notes. (Oct 21st) Met Bill & Eleanor & grandma coming home. They wanted to come home for tea not go to Eve's.

[At top of page] 'Letters of T.E. Lawrence'. Mostly to men. Warm hearted but interested in things. Only once longs for a little home life. Great width & depth of knowledge.

Thursday, 16 October

Cold and wettish. Collected rations in afternoon. Eggs, baked beans, chocolate. Up to Library to change books.

Friday, 17 October
Not bad day. Cleaned kitchen & scullery.

Sunday, 19 October
Chi went to S. School. Bill slightly averse. Went for walk after tea round Herdman's fields. Frank in when we returned.

[At top of page] Collection of poetry by living poets.

Monday. 20 October
Bill woke me early mother dear. Ate very little breakfast. Ready for School half an hour before time. Took him down to Council Infants. Miss Hall (HT) delighted him by calling him Billy. He never noticed me leave the Babies Room. Busy looking round. Goodbye my baby son. Returned home for dinner complete with large scratch on cheek. Girl gave him it but for why can't discover. The Gill's boys take him to school but he races back with Clifford (Pears) over the 'Rockies'.

Tuesday, 21 October
Autumn Council Meeting Bishop Auckland. Mrs. Johnson & Mrs. Forster there. Good Companions. Me complete with delegate's badge declaring Leadgate to the staring world. Noisy Meeting in Cinema. Women on stage very inaudible. Man Doctor spoke to his boots. Delegate to Oxford read amusing & interesting account. Woman who had lived in U.S.A. gave good talk. Tried to educate us on History but everyone delighted in her life there. Left gas mask in cinema. Only discovered on walking up Elm Terr.

Wednesday, 22 October
Bill enthusiastic about school. Scarcely has time for dinner. Recites poem about a little house. Reads Ella's books. Knows alphabet pictures & words. Num-bers up to 10. Miss Love (teacher) has won him. Writes C for cat.

Thursday, 23 October

Bill asks what makes mist on plane (propeller?) Thinks it will tickle the feet of God & Jesus. Will they laugh? Eleanor plays with Helen Seymour but has hectic moments with Bill when available. Misses him very much. Noticeable in temperamental outbursts. Oranges with rations 2 lbs 1/3½.

Friday, 24 October

Bill hears that Clifford eats cabbage. Tells me he can eat it now when he is five. Good. He recites poem with actions. She (He) curtsied low to me. Takes hold of trousers & nearly puts knot in legs. Called at Mrs. Turnbull's shop. Could hardly leave. Long History of British Women's Legion Secretaryship Mrs. S. Turnbull suggested me for President. Others supported her!! Feel rather helpless, Che sera sera.

Saturday, 25 October

Fine sunny day. Caught 1 pm. bus to Durham. Plenty of room (surprising). Then got bus to B. Auckland. Lovely sun. Bus full. Bill wanted seat but had to be content with one of my knees. Eleanor on other. Bought him a cap for school. Saw dark ruby red coat I fancied. No price on. Recovered gas mask. Walked in Palace Park. Picked fallen leaf. Trees glorious. Rich patchwork of colours. Home by 7 pm.

Sunday, 26 October

Cold windy. Chi went to S. School quietly. Did not feel like walk. Frank down in evening. Ella will only get 3 days leave but will combine it with 2 days weekend. Wrote to U.S.A., Ella, Mrs. Crouch (10/-) Will.

Monday, 27 October

Fine bright morning wind N by NW (So I think) Washed bedclothes etc. but did not dry so well as expected. Dampish towards afternoon. Collected allowance.

[Crossed out] John walked in with book Told Bill he had not to touch it or look at it. Fool that I am, I flamed out at him after keeping my mouth shut for 2 yrs. Now Eve will [End of crossing out]

10 Woodbines, 2 ½ Cadbury Choc. At Boustead's. 5 Woodbines at McAloon's. Pictures at night. Good Merchant Seaman picture.

Tuesday, 28 October

Cold N.E. wind. Dusted kitchen bedrooms & stairs. Then ironed washing. Mother at Store in morning. Then visited friend in Castleside in afternoon. Eve down after tea. Asked for Mother. Went upstairs to lav. Spoke to Eleanor & departed. Letter from Will. Very well but lonely. Mrs. Kettlewell still there. Doesn't think he can manage Xmas presents.

Wednesday, 29 October

Bitter N.E. Wind. Sudden storms of snow. Bright sunny intervals. Wind died down later in evening. Whist Drive at Mrs. Telford's, 2pm. Only 8 attended. Proceeds for Seamen. Bill excited at snow. Anxious to get out instead of having dinner. Eleanor made 'Popeyes'. Overlooked Eleanor's kilt. Time for women's clothes. Lined Bill's helmet. Stitched Clean covers on cushions. Started Bill a jersey. Heard at W. Drive that Church has been robbed on Sunday. After Harvest Gifts (£40) but it was not there.

Saturday, 1 November

Letter from Joan. Leave cut short so did not call here. Sent tartan match holder. Where are the books of matches now?

Monday, 3 November

Wire from William reminding me of Nov 5th. Sent him wire back.

Tuesday, 4 November

Washed some of chi's things. Dried rather well.

Wednesday, 5 November

Fine but cold. Sent Eleanor down to McAloon's for bread, 1 large or 2 small. Brought all 3 back. Made sandwiches cut up Fruit and Malt loaf. Biscuits for refreshments at Whist Drive. Only 5 here. But made 10/- all told. Some members sent money. So agreed to send 30/- to Seamen's Fund. Kept 3/- for Hut Fund. Mrs. Dixon came over to say she couldn't stay as Company had moved. Stayed over 1 hr. Fred (her man in navy) written & by bits told her he was in Malta, expects to see Phoebe Henderson's man in Ark Royal.

[At top of page] 'Thus Germany Spoke – Collection of Scraps': to show that the blame of the war rests on all Germany not just Hitler.

Friday, 7 November

Wet day. Cleaned kitchen etc. Bought myself pair of stockings at Grainger's.

Saturday, 8 November

Hard frost, ground white. But Sunny. Sold Poppies over the Railways. Such nice people clean nice houses on the whole. Real Leadgate people. Not like Bungalows. But nearly frozen. Dinner at 2.30 had a little whisky in my tea and 2 aspirin.

Sunday, 9 November

Quiet day Walk down Durham Rd. Bill turned back. Rained heavily at night. Frank down (½lb b(utter?).)

Monday, 10 November

Windy day early changed to rain. Did not wash. Felt lazy. School hours 9.15–12.15, 1.15–3.30. Raining so went to meet Bill. Boy came out to be sick. Hope he is not sickening for anything. Poor kid.

Tuesday, 11 November

Cold. Did a little washing but did not dry as day damp but fine & sunny. Mrs. Hardy afraid it is a weather breeder. Went down to school to meet Bill. Had to chase him up Front St. Caught him up outside Italian ice cream Shop hesitating whether to follow his mates. He didn't. Called in Turnbull's shop afterwards with Fruit Preservation Book. Gossiped. Scandalised. Mrs. Pickering had gone to Mrs. Dixon's for tea last Wed. That was the company that arrived.

Wednesday, 12 November

Cold & windy. Eleanor's eyes running with mucus. Full of cold. Winked castor oil into them & it has cleared the stuff out. Cleaned bedrooms. Lovely sunny afternoon. Bill got lost in middle of Polly Flinders & I helped him out. "How do you know it?" said he. Search for my Ration Book. Looked for another green one like the chi's. Forgot it was white. Bill started Sums today. Very proud of himself. 2 + 1 = 3. Will say mix not makes.

[At top of page] 'Glorious Adventure' – Halliburton (Greek wanderings) 'Women & Children Last' – B. Nichols. 'The Road to Nowhere' – Maurice Walsh (Irish)

Thursday, 13 November

Wet & windy & cold. Went for rations before dinner. Collected two 20's cigs Boustead's & Hopper's. Good. Hope I don't have to fall back on Woodbines. Changed libraries in afternoon. Spent so long had to hurry home. Eleanor's eyes still running. Points Books collected. Mr. Brown home over the road. Saw him & her and was shocked to see the miserable unhappy look on her face. Lot of gossip about them both. Will my face shock anyone when My Man comes home with its radiance? Scribbled lines about faith & love.

Friday, 14 November

Cold but fine. Mother went up to Eve's early on. Eleanor & I cleaned up. Her eyes are much better but cried with earache at dinner time. Warm olive oil & half aspirin cured it. Bill did more sums. Played school all night. I was teacher, Eleanor mummy. Mother saw man Killed at bus stand. Wrote out lines to Faith. Post to N/C. J[ournal] tomorrow. Ark Royal sunk.[13] Poor Phoebe H. and all the other wives. God help them.

Saturday, 15 November

Cold enough. Eleanor seems better but eats very slowly as if throat is tender. Went up to Consett in afternoon. Paid 3/11 for Bill a flannelette shirt. Grey. Let's hope it doesn't look black after one day at school. Talk with Ethel (Walker) Seymour. Both Margaret & Helen had mumps. Now severe colds. Am afraid we were guilty of talking big about our chi. Margaret can do sums like 5 + 4 = 9 without counting. Sunny afternoon. Bill & I had run down Durham Rd with Snip. Letter from Ella. Only 1 casualty on Ark Royal. 1600 men.

Sunday, 16 November

Bitterly cold day. Hard frost early on. Softened to rain at teatime. Eleanor seemed a lot better but had a dose of earache at dinner time, then was lively till 8 pm. Bill was O.K. I do hope Eleanor is not sickening for anything, mumps?

Monday, 17 November

Looked fine morning but soon turned to rain. Did not wash. Eleanor seems a little better. Certainly eating better. Bill talking thickly but eating well. Fair afternoon. Eleanor went to P.O. with me.

Tuesday, 18 November

Fine day. Lovely sunshine. Washed and ironed after tea. Very tired but pictures soothing. Very little sense of criticism left. Just accept what the gods send in the way of entertainment and am seldom bored. Eleanor out in sunshine with grandma. British Forces advance on 120m. front into Libya. Aim to destroy enemy's tanks & armoured defences. Not announced till Thurs.

Wednesday, 19 November

Fine day again. Sunshine doing overtime. Eleanor went up to Consett with grandma in morning. In afternoon went to Church M.U. meeting. I went to Women's Institute meeting. Elected as Committee Member. Woman eager to see me Presi[dent] not there – Miss Hall proposed Mrs. D. remain as P. Nobody seconded but no other nomination. All sat like stuffed cabbages(?) Just sheep. Will go home & grumble. Mrs. Hunter Executive Councillor present complimented me on fine report of Autumn Council & interested in American letter.

Memo: Russians still keeping up magnificent front. Serious round Tula. Kerch occupied by Germans. Making desperate effort.

Thursday, 20 November

Letter from B/mth. Misty moisty day. After tidying up kitchen, dusted washed out bedrooms & bathroom thoroughly. Do until Spring. Wash curtains & windows next week. Handed in grocery order. Mr. Ogle brought things up later. Bill & Eleanor spent evening cutting out. Floor littered but it kept them busy. Eve down for tea. Again ate only cake. Afraid to use butter? Says they have nothing in house to eat. No jam for this month. Let her have 1 lb & ½ lb marg. Doesn't look grand. Can't understand her?

Friday, 21 November

Wet sort of day. Bill landed home at tea time dripping but laughing. Mother up at Eve's. Cleaned up kitchen & scullery. Hope it's fine next week to take up carpet & whitewash ceiling. Very dusty. Pictures at night. Linked up with Lily McDonald. Red headed Irish woman.

Saturday, 22 November

Wet morning. Postponed trip to Newcastle again for photos. Throat feels tight. Eleanor & Bill O.K. Took flowers up to Father. 3 white Chrysanths 1/- filled out with privet. Watched wedding group come out of church. Did you marry my daddy says Bill. Was that when I wasn't here? Was I only a little wee seed in the ground says he, or was I beside God?

Sunday, 23 November

Damp misty day. Throat feels a little better. Chi at S. School while I had a nap. Frank down after tea. Mother at Eve's. Advance into Libya going well. Battle still raging but R.A.F. & our tanks proving superior. Germans held in triangle Sollum, El Gubi Tobruk. 10/- to B/mth.

[At top of page] 'Words Win Wars' – J. Hargraves. Call for better propaganda as a weapon of war. 'Savoy, Corsica, Tunis' – B. Newman. 'Chaffinch' [sic] – H.W. Freeman.

Monday, 24 November

Windy but damp no drying. Washed net curtains from bedrooms. Washed window frames. Eleanor helped. Collected pay at P.O. Mrs. Pickering retired, niece postmistress now. Up to Consett library to change books with Eleanor. Still no mechanical toys. Bill's Xmas stocking going to be poor. Meeting of L.W.W.P. in Guildhall. Concert Sunday night first Door to Door sale of tickets. Mrs. Crosby spent night with mother & I went to pictures.

Tuesday, 25 November

Fine sunny day. Mrs. Hardy calls it another weather breeder. Mother decided to bake so could not take up carpet, but washed scullery walls & cleaned shelf. Mrs. Proudlock's son ill again. Taken to Murray's Hospital for operation for appendicitis but not put through. Discovered Bill had spots at bath time. Chickenpox?

Wednesday, 26 November

High N.E. wind. Called in Doctor McIntyre. Confirmed my opinion. Chicken Pox. Bill not really invalid. Enjoyed breakfast in bed. Not much dinner but good tea & supper. Written our B[lack] B[oar]d with chalks, read books, coloured pictures. Eleanor pleased to have him at home. Given 12 1/- & 6 9d tickets to sell for Sunday night concert.

Thursday, 27 November

Weather cold wettish. Cleaned windows. Dusted bedrooms. Bill inclined to itch. Chalked all day. Made him some 'sum' cards. Did them without a flicker. 1+1= , 2+2 = , 2+1= , 3+1 = . Drawings. Coloured books. Copied words. Eleanor did her best to imitate. Impossible to isolate him in this tiny house. Eleanor went shopping with me for rations. Got Mother Goose & Sleeping Beauty to read to them. Bill wants to go to school, just a few spots not 'Chicken Fox'. Won't know what Miss Lowe's tells chi. stories, sums, etc. Promised to go down to ask her.

Friday, 28 November

Miss Keenleyside [?] died. Xmas Card from Will today (posted Oct 28.) Weather fine & sunny quite mild. Bill & Eleanor in garden while I cleaned up. Later both come in to polish for me. Take Bill (& E.) to see Doctor. Doing well. Another brother from Wed. says Bill wears too many clothes. His son in S. America near Cape Horn runs round in next to nothing. Harder than mother. These boys must take the place of the men who are killed. Lunched well or would have thought Bill's father might be one of those men. Boasting of his son safe in S. Am. We have no draught-proof houses or schools. Can't buy the best clothes so must wear more. No maybe it was just drink.

Saturday, 29 November

Raining all day. Bill much better. Spots dying. Marion Hall ill. Mrs. Ogle whispered that it was Fever but she could stay at home as she was only one. Bill says he has a sergeant's back when someone remarks on his straight back. He also says "B for bat and Bot". Eleanor & he played round all day and been very pally. Sold 12/9 worth of tickets this afternoon for Concert. Got 2 lbs oranges at McAloon's. Stitched up Bill's red & navy jersey.

Sunday, 30 November

Took chi down to Annfield Plain to Maggie's. Enjoyed ourselves. Young Herbert's friends in for tea. Did not return in time for concert.

Monday, 1 December

Washing Day. Clothes dried fine. Meeting for L.W.W.P. to discuss Boxing Day Fancy Dress Carnival for chi, afternoon. Whist Drive & Dance at night. Meeting rushed for most ladies were due at Vicarage for M. Union Whist & Ambulance man due for Hall for their class. Mother won first prize 185. Very proud of herself. Never done it before. Chose Rabbit rather than dressing table set.

Tuesday, 2 December

Good day, windy & cold. Baking Day. Rabbit pie for dinner. Lovely. Mother took some over to Mrs. Lax and she actually ate some. Poor soul, no appetite, no sleep, painful legs.

Sunday, 7 December

Not bad day. Mother's friend from Castleside down for tea & supper. Good company. Frank called for an hour. Discovered Eleanor has half a doz. spots.

[At top of page] 'Not I, but the Wind' – Frieda Lawrence. (D.H.L. wife) Historical novel? Small talk.

Monday, 8 December

Japan attacked U.S.A. in Pacific. Fine day. So hoisted carpet after Mother left for Eve's. Whitened ceiling. More successful this time. Not such a mess on furniture & walls but floor splashed. Eleanor & Bill quite enjoyed it. Alarm 6 pm-ish for half an hour. Went to pictures. Alarm later 10.30 pm. to 12.30 am. Very heavy thuds, windows rattled. Too tired to stay up so to bed 12 pm. Eleanor's spots developing.

Tuesday, 9 December

Sent Will a wire. Fine day again. Finished off as much as possible but like old woman, all aches & pains. Polished furniture after washing it. Eve down, says bomb dropped in Gill Wood. Not far off, but some say it did not explode. Hung my pictures, 'Laughing Cavalier' & 'When did you last see your father'? Chi very interested. Is it a lady? Is it a man? What's he wearing those things for? Eleanor's spots inflamed – itching. Wakens through the night.

Wednesday, 10 December

Took things easily. Eleanor out of sorts but still eating well.

Memo: While Jap. Was in Washington on a mission, the Japs attacked Honolulu Pearl Harbour,[14] Philippines Wake Island Hong Kong Malay Pen. etc. War declared by U.S.A. on Japan. Germany declared war on U.S.A.

Thursday, 11 December

Cold & wind. Dusted house quickly. Mother went off to town. Did not tell her of W.I. Committee meeting or she would not have gone. Went over to Mrs. Telford to tell her I couldn't go. Had quite a gossip there. Just finished tea when mother arrived tired cold & hungry. So off I went with Mrs. T. to Medomsley Edge. Only 2 members absent. Miss Hall elected Sec. Me Vice President. President gave Sec. a look as if to say that wasn't what we planned. Many undercurrents. Miss Hall advised me to apply for Temp. Teaching.

Friday, 12 December

Cold wind. Some sun. Cleaned kitchen. Dusted bedrooms & stairs. Collected rations. 10 eggs! Chi allowed 4 each now. Ordered sirloin from Butcher.

Saturday, 13 December

Windy but fine. Cleaned up. Did a little shopping for cake. Went to pictures. What would I do without pictures?

Sunday, 14 December

Quiet day, Heavy rainfall. No-one called. In all day. Started to knit dress for Eleanor's doll.

[At top of page] 'The Flying Visit' – P. Fleming. Hitler in England – cabinet did not know what to do with him so returned him to Germany.

Monday, 15 December

Raining morning. Cleared in afternoon. Bill not at school because of cough & slight cold. Wish he could go. Too boisterous for small house. Eleanor's spots dying rapidly. Collected pay. Posted 10/- to B/mth. Insurance money. MSS to Lilliput. Card to Will. Library Consett. Called at Frank's to pay up Club. Asked for doll. Told none had been put away. Terribly disappointed. Got one 1/6 but not so pretty & does not go to sleep.

Tuesday, 16 December

Fine wind but very slow drying. Washed. Mother baked pasties and bread buns. Eve & John down after tea. John very pale. Bill's tank in pieces when he left. Went to pictures. Bill had bad fit of coughing 1.30 pm. Finished bonnet & dress for Eleanor's doll.

Wednesday, 17 December

Wire from Will. Xmas greetings. Sunny but cold & Dry. Stitched & pressed doll's frock & bonnet. Cleaned up. Prepared dinner. Mother down to Shotley for afternoon so chi accompanied me to W.I. More than usual. Mrs. Ashby spoke on forces in the world combined to unify & harmonise the people. Meeting of Jam Committee fixed for Tues. 6 pm. Alarm 6 pm (ish) to 8 pm (ish). Busy ironing. Heard nothing But Mrs. Gill says Works Hooter went.

[At top of page] 'Scoop' by E. Waugh – Journalists foreign correspondents.

Thursday, 18 December

Fine sunny frosty day, bitterly cold morning. Took Bill to Town with me. Gave me his masculine advice quite free & quite freely. Chose pink hanky for grandma. Paid up for it later like a gent. Little to choose. Most presents for millionaires. Canadian soldiers sat at our table for lunch. Worked on C.P.R. on Royal Train during Tour. King knew he was familiar when inspecting Troops. Spent 24/6 on little things. Bill thrilled to shake hands with Father Xmas but not embarrassed. Huge tree in Central. Good day. Bill fine company.

Friday, 19 December

Cold. Cleaned out kitchen & scullery. Went shopping with chi. Bought Xmas Tree. Spent evening decorating kitchen. Most of streamers & toys for tree come from Valletta. No Will here to do the decorating. Always will remember when he decorated for

Billy first day up after measles 1938. His face lit up with delight. Posted Xmas parcels.

Saturday, 20 December

Cold dampish. In afternoon went for groceries. Must not leave it so late again.

Sunday, 21 December

Quiet day. Bill restless. Frank down in evening. Thought he might go to Darlington on Xmas Day. Not come here.

[At top of page] 'Augustus St. [sic] John Drawings'. H.M. Morton [sic – H.V. Morton], 'Our fellow men'. Sketches of ordinary man.

Monday, 22 December

Not bad day. Did a little washing. Collected pay at P.O. Left order at W. Wilson's.

Tuesday, 23 December

Ironed, cleaned etc. Collected Train set etc, bought a few more hankies at Consett. Lent Betty Lax coupons to buy presents. Changed library Books. Left toys next door as Bill saw me coming.

Wednesday, 24 December

Cold. Did Friday's work today. Shopping in afternoon. 1 lb oranges each child. Chocolate. Children on best behaviour. Want to sleep downstairs. Finished woollies for doll Looks quite sweet. Filled stockings. S.A. carols singers round.

Memo: Chi. Presents. Grandma Crouch. 5/- each Savings Card. Joan & Cyril same. Frank same. Ron & Elsye Blocks. George & Queen Books. Ella, stockings. Toys Book. Eve & Ralph Toy soldiers & planes, Paints, Chocolates.

Churchill in Washington for Conference with Roosevelt.

[At top of page] 'Fire over England' – A.E. Mason. [Queen] Elizabeth [I] & [King] Philip [II of Spain]. [Book about the Spanish Armada].

Thursday, 25 December
Bill disappointed no snow. A merry Xmas for the children. Thrilled with their toys. Train set for Bill. Told me later that the wheels were made to come off. Doll for Eleanor. Not called Elizabeth Jane. Her Baby Girl & called Baby. Stockings filled with Orange, nuts, chocolate, hankie, Shop stocking & cracker. Very nice dinner, pork (hardly a joint 1/10) carrots, spinach potatoes, onion stuffing, Xmas pudding (small but delicious). Mother went off to Scotswood for tea. George in India. 4 hrs in shelter last week gave Auntie Cold. Alarm 5.30–6.30 (ish).

Friday, 26 December
My Wedding Anniversary. Seven Years Wed. but scarcely 3½ yrs of married life. I seem to have always had to carry on alone. Eleanor pulled doll's leg off. Children's Carnival very rough. Children impossible. Bill & Eleanor frightened of the noise. Whist Drive & Dance packed. Over £14 cash at door. Refreshments in great demand. Very tired. So many helpers who thought they were doing more than their share.

Saturday, 27 December
Quiet day, tired. Not much shopping to do. Eve Ralph & John down for tea. Bitterly cold, Hard white frost.

Sunday, 28 December
Bitterly cold. Frost never gave all day. Frank down in evening. Mended Doll. Played with chi. Forgot to take present with him. Only 2 hankies & tub of Shaving Cream. Brought me 40 cigs.

Monday, 29 December

Frost given. Good wind. Washed but not all dried. Went to pictures. Stayed in when Siren went, but came home soon. Enemy planes overhead. Bombs dropped at Greencroft. Mother in a shake. Children slept. 8.30–10.30 pm. Letter from U.S.A. today. Thinks my hubby looks handsome & distinguished just their idea of an Englishman. Sent dime for Billy. Another for Eleanor coming. Showed my letter round to women.

Tuesday, 30 December

Fine day. Not so cold. Ironed in evening. Went to Eve's for the afternoon. Enjoyed ourselves quietly. Children really got on together for once.

Wednesday, 31 December

Fine day again. Cleaned kitchen & bedrooms & stairs etc in morning. Put washing away. After dinner went up to Castleside to Mrs. Jackson's for tea. Chi achieved ambition to ride on top of Double Decker. Very good. Quiet gossipy time. Daughter married to George Turnbull. Used to belong to Tennis Club in days of my youth. Returned to Consett. Went to Empire Cinema. Home 9.20 pm. Chi dead tired. Waiting now to let Old Year out & New Year in with Mother. John Lax is first foot. Cake & ginger wine are ready.

Memo: Churchill visited Canada.

1942

[Here follows her diary for 1942 written in ink in a notebook.
It is incomplete and ends in March.]

Thursday, 1 January

After tidying up the kitchen to greet the new broom listened to Big Ben chiming the death of 1941 with mother. John Lax, black hair, nearly black eyes, dark skin, put first foot over our threshold at 12.2 pm. Brought a nice 'roundie' (piece of coal). Wished us all A Happy New Year. He cut the cake cleanly (good luck) and in extremely generous slices, considering everything, but maybe that signifies a generous giving and receiving year. It was rather hard to cut. John was afraid for the knife. No nuts, no icing. We all toasted the New Year in homemade ginger wine (nearly burnt my throat). After a stiff forced kind of conversation (e.g. By isn't he growing now? How old are ye John?) our first foot had to leave to perform the ceremony at Hannah's and his grandmother's and then be up at 5 am for work. That first greeting from the first foot always makes my throat swell with emotion. I remember my first New Year away from home. I was very merry & bright over Xmas, but the instant I heard the bells ringing in the New Year & the buzzers blowing, I felt surging up within me the longing for my father & mother's fireside and I cried. No-one knew what was the matter. They were all Southerners but my husband-to-be understood a little and comforted me. It is the feeling of facing the unknown that draws families together, a fear of standing alone and helpless before the inexorable executioner, Time. It was a fine open day and Bill & Eleanor spent the whole day outside playing, for which I was thankful. No grand dinner. Butcher sent 1 sheep's heart and 3 mutton chops but they did not cook in time (oven sulky) so we had potato hot pot made from a little meat left over from yesterday and semolina and raisins pudding. Jelly (beaten up with white of egg) & custard (using up yolk) for tea but Bill did not fancy jelly. Mother went out for tea with Mrs. N. Starkey then called at Annfield Plain for supper. I washed some woollies out after tea. Quiet night knitting a helmet for Bill. Letter from 'Chan', Malta dated Nov. 14th '41. Thanks for Xmas presents, card & letter. Says Will is kicking his heels to return to us. Mrs. Taylor had baby boy. So all women can't be evacuated. Regrets returned to me. If I had stayed I would have been with my love and not have been separated all these long 2½ years. That 'if'.

[Note at top of page] Read 'Brave New World' – A. Huxley. Fascinating theory but horrifying.

'With Allenby in Palestine [and Lawrence in Arabia] – Lovell Sherman. [sic – directed by Lowell Thomas] Made a Hero of Todd Colney. Very little of T.E.L.[15]

'Our Fellow Men' – H.V. Morton. Not so interesting as his travel books.

Friday, 2 January

Fine day again. Some wind and dampness but pleasant. Chi out most of the day. The kitchen needed the same cleaning as any Friday despite Wednesday's work. Such a dusty, sooty house. Blame these big open fireplaces that need so much cleaning.

Friday, 9 January

Eve's birthday. 38. Looks awful but I can't credit it as a fact. Never think of ages. Bill began school again on Tuesday and is a tough 'big' boy again. Very proud to tell me he is in the top section. He took a book round to all the teachers recited their names one by one. Miss Green inquired his name. Did you take it to Miss Hall said I. He laughed at me. Of course not. She's not a teacher. What is she then? She's there to smack the naughty boys and girls and to give the boys & girls that are late the cane. Miss H. is Head Teacher.

While talking to Norman D. about America being so unprepared for Japan's attack, he said, "If you give another man your coat, you can't keep warm yourself."

Nothing has been mentioned of Churchill for a day or two. (It seems like a week to me.)

Germans attacked a convoy early this week in Atlantic. 3 subs. sunk and planes brought down. Very little damage to convoy compared with its size.

Hope these last two facts are unconnected.

Malta has been repeatedly raided. On Wednesday reported 10 raids in 24 hrs. At weekend our planes from Malta raided Sicilian airfield, did damage to troop carriers & troops waiting to set off for Libya. Wire from Will last Sunday. O.K. Eleanor's doll lost the other leg but Freddie lad Crosby mended it in a fashion. Eleanor is scared to lift the poor thing. She sings Away in a Manger beautifully. Bill has no time. Snow fell on Wednesday, Thursday & Friday. Not much. Enough for chi to have a little sledging. Bill rather timid but wants his own sledge.

I've developed a heavy head cold but Eleanor rummaging in drawer (as she loves) discovered a tube of inhalant that has cleared my head marvellously. Think it's staved off flue [sic].

Meeting of W.I. committee. Next meeting seems to be mine. I provide refreshment for speakers, and the mystery prize and conduct the Sing Song or pay Entertainment. Only hope I can waken a response in those solid women.

Eve had a letter from Ella Thurs. expects to be home for the weekend. Had a letter from Mrs. Hoferbier USA She sent a dime for Bill, another for Eleanor. Has shown the snaps I sent her to her friends and to women at the Agriculturists' Conference (or something). They all think Will is handsome & distinguished, just what they thought an English man would look like Ahem. The children are sweet. No mention of Mother! I will take it as complimentary, so there.

Tuesday, 13 January

Ella arrived on Sat. Frank had met her, train was 1½ hrs. late. She grows more, how shall I put – always-been-waited-on-all-my-life-ish. Still £4 a week job is bound to give an air of confident, expectant, comfort.

[At top of page] Books – 'Journal of Katherine Mansfield', 'The Holy Tenor' – H.G. Wells, 'In the Master's Footsteps' – H.V. Morton.

She brought a gorgeous pork pie, nearly the size of a tea plate and we gorged ourselves on it. Eve and John came down and we were an overcrowded gobbling roomful. I escaped to the pictures after preparing the children for bed. They were thrilled to be taken to bed by Auntie. Sunday was quieter. Needless to say I was late for breakfast but did not get the lie-in suggested to cure my cold. Ella & Eleanor went out before dinner, first to father's grave, then to Ross's where they had some wine & cake. Eleanor did not eat much dinner. Bill cleaned his plate after a romp in the snow. Frank did not arrive till 5.15 pm. We had had tea. Ella had waited. I can't understand him. He doesn't act like an eager lover at all. Of course he is 35 yrs old (I think) but both seem to hold back from each other, as if they are afraid of letting each other see that they are keen. Yet they have 'gone together' (as we say) for ten years or thereabouts. Time they faced facts. If the fact they are of different religions prevents Ella from marrying him, or the fact that he is rather chesty (so I think) why don't they part finally? Is it just pure cussedness? They never give each other presents (because of something one of them said about one long ago, I believe). She has been away for six months and as far as I know, he has never attempted to see her. Yet he is in decent work and could have afforded the trip to Bolton I'm sure. But what's the use of an outsider talking? When an Irishman and a Redhead will neither bend nor break, what's to be done?

Ella was talking again of the low type of woman in the factory. Such animal-like features, coarse vulgar ways and impossible language. Terrible to be thrown among it without warning. One girl, about 20 yrs, sweet and nice, cried and cried for days. Every body sympathised & comforted her, thinking it was home-sickness, but she confided later she was terrified of the women she was working with.

Quite a blizzard last night. Snow driving & whipping into my face. Could not see far in the dark. Continued to fall Today but wind died down & snow thawed as it fell. Chi out after tea and came with soaking wet rubber boots. I must not let such little things upset me. Wet feet if attended to will not cause their deaths nor will they trouble me more than I let them.

The siren sounded twice today. Just after 11 am for 15 minutes and again at 3.30 pm-ish till 4 pm-ish. Heard nothing but News announced bombs had fallen in N.E. and some people killed. It is an unreal life, a horrid incredible nightmare of a life, that while we wait nervously and tensely for the All Clear some-one is being shattered and scattered into eternity, simply because an unknown man has pressed a button.

Saturday, 17 January

Chief item of news today is the return of Churchill. He arrived at 11 am at Paddington Station greeted by the Cabinet and wife. Had flown from Bermuda to Plymouth accompanied by Beaverbrook and Sir Dudley Pounds. What a prize crew for the Nazis. Journey took 18 hrs. Little short of a miracle to me, but to the next generation maybe a joke, just as the speed of the first locomotive or car is to us. Each generation seems to have its own perspective. Sense of proportion is more important in the teaching of history than dates. The marvel or the terror of today quickly wilts under the contempt of tomorrow. The raids of the Danes & Anglo Saxons must have kept the poor people on our coast & up the rivers in a constant state of alarm. Their ears must have been constantly strained to hear the raid alarm. The Norman invasion & the intended Spanish invasion must have raised the same anxiety, the same burning determination to fight as the Nazis have raised today. It has all happened before, only with different details and in growing proportions – the fight for mastery so that one group of people should lord it over the rest. Whoever won or lost, there was always a conquering people. Will it be like that this time? If the New World is really being born that cannot be. We must merge into one great World Family with a world outlook, a world policy, a worldwide scheme of economics, finance, education. The ordinary man is ready for it, waiting for it, eager for it. It is the only way to secure peace. No more patriotism, frontiers, duties, etc., but no deadly uniform sameness in every land. People must develop in their own way, keep their own language, customs, songs & dances, their own peculiarities, the kind of work they can do best. But educated to respect the individuality of other peoples. Can that be? Yes, if the rising generation is educated in the right way. It cannot change us, my generation, not in a night at least. All our lives we will remember the German air aids, the Italian fleet safe in home waters, the French surrender, the Japs' stealthy attack under cover of deceit.

But it must be seen to that our children grow up with their minds looking out on the world, not turned inwards to the home fireside. Consideration, respect, and mutual admiration and help must take the place of 'Land of Hope and Glory' and 'The British Navy' etc. That can only be done by education.

My belief is that Education is the Root of all evil and the Cure of all evil.

Anyway, I'm glad Churchill is back. I have been worried. Who could replace him at present?

Bill has been interested in the question of where babies come from. He accepted my suggestion of being a seed in God's garden waiting to grow, last year after watching the growth of garden stuff from seeds to carrots, parsnips, peas, etc. Now he is trying to make Eleanor accept his belief. I heard her proclaiming " I wasn't a seed. I was a baby girl." Today he wants to know "What makes you talk?" If he had been older, I would have said, "generally an absence of ideas and facts, rarely knowledge". Instead I tried to tell him he had a voice box in his throat, showed him where to feel his what-do-you-call-it? He has felt it carefully ever since and kept talking just to feel it moving & vibrating. But, he asked, "what happens to your box when your food goes down. Doesn't it get filled up?" He couldn't grasp the idea of it shutting with no-one to touch the lid, so we finally agreed that the food slipped down the side. He has also discovered this week that Miss Hall is the Head Teacher to smack the naughty children at the desk. "Go to the desk you naughty boy." Is a terrifying command. I know. It gave me an empty hollow feeling in the middle. And when I was caned (very rarely, I was too scared to be a nuisance) I always felt the pain most in my stomach.

I wrote to Mrs. Hoferbier, Portsmouth, Iowa, U.S.A. "The whole world is our village today. Why, I have even got a neighbour in Portsmouth, Iowa! Is that not one of the wonders of our time? … The fact that we can write to each other so freely and neighbourly two people of different nations, so very far apart and completely unknown to each other is surely important. It is a sign of the times; the writing on the wall, only this time it is on paper." I sent in my application for a job as supply teacher on Thursday 15th. Sent Will's mother 10/- this week.

Friday, 23 January

What a week, what a week. If Heaven there be, surely the Master Craftsman will have many stern rebukes to administer to the men who designed or passed the designs or built Council Houses.

1. Bathroom too cold to use in winter because hot tank is downstairs, ours, an end house, built over the coalhouse and thin flooring allows the penetration of frost & wind to say nothing of badly fitted doors and windows.
2. I discover tonight by way of a burst that the pipes travel through the pantry on the way to or from the bathroom to the scullery, and here there Is no way of keeping the pipes warm except by removing certain foods and keeping a lamp or something burning there.
3. In the summer the sun penetrates grudgingly into the kitchen, which is also the living room, for little more than an hour in the morning, but shines lovingly all day long on the very window that should be in the shade, the pantry window.
4. The scullery sink and taps are in a dark corner.
5. Not one door fits. Not one window that does not rattle and allow wind to blow the snow, rain, frost.

The weather this week has been severe. I washed on Monday and Tuesday morning found the pipes in the bathroom frozen. Using the gas, candle in plant pot and primus stove, I thawed all out except the hot taps. Left the gas & candle burning all night. Next morning all frozen again. Thawed them out again but Thursday discovered the hot pipe had left the tap joint. The plumber sent a lad to look it over. He turned the water off and promised to return but when, oh Lord, when?

I daren't have too big a fire although the boiler flue is blocked and mother has had to sit over the fire all week. Today she has worn a coat. But today a thaw has set in. It has rained steadily all day and the 'locals' said at first, "It's freezing as it comes down." No they could not see how impossible that is. (Is it?) As I see it, the rain meets the frozen surface and is itself turned to ice for a while by the intense cold or maybe it washes the top snow off and reveals the ice beneath. The first seems more practicable. Anyway the outside walls, the railings, the roads and pavements were sheeted with ice this morning, but it was broken up and melting quickly this evening. The spouts are running especially those that need repairing near our coal house door and Mrs. Gill's back door. A bitter wind has blown all the week from Monday night and snow has been in great drifts. Bus routes have been blocked the High Stables the Hat & Feather and the Lond, three highest points round Leadgate, had drifts six feet high. Thank God it has started to thaw so quickly, but this will not mean the end of winter. It's only the beginning, but the frost might not be so severe again.

The News this week is not very heartening either.

1. The Japs are advancing on Singapore and preparing to land on islands near Australia. They are still held in Luzon but there doesn't seem much hope there.

2. Rommel has advanced and retaken Jedabaya in Libya. To think that all the men who have fought and died to drive him twice back across Libya may have died in vain is not to be permitted. I can't bear it.

3. Hundreds of Nazi planes are stored near West European coast ready for a Spring offensive. So our paper says.

4. One bright, very glad side to the war is the Russian advance against the Nazis. They are beyond Mojaiski now. They seem determined to play Hitler's game and win. One opponent at a time. Finish the Nazis, then turn on the Japs. And I feel a growing belief that they will do this and the world will owe Russia an everlasting debt of gratitude. I only hope certain people can say, Thank You and others, Pleased to have been of service.

I have sent Will a telegram today. I dreamed of him last night, thought he came in here so quietly and did not follow me up to bed for a long time. When he did, Billy awoke and knew him at once but he never spoke. My very dear. He looked well, stronger and tougher in spirit, but none of his robust, high spirited fire. What will the years have done to him? Turned his boy's heart into a man's of course, but maybe more. God keep him.

Friday, 20 March

I have been very lazy little book, or too taken up with other things to record the fleeting hours.

February was remarkable for many things in the history of the World, but I may be forgiven for recording here an event of breathtaking importance to me. I saw myself in print! Three of my poems (I may call them that for want of a better word or from personal vanity, which?) were approved of by the Editor of Consett & Stanley Chronicle, Durham County? & Bishop Auckland Chronicle. True he asked permission to print them and no mention was made of a cheque. I suppose I should rejoice purely in the recognition of my art. It must be true that all poets starve in the early stages of this journey to fame. The poems were: 'As I sit alone', 'A Woman's Prayer' & 'Salute to Malta'. I really must state here that Miss ?, I forget her name, at the Bring & Buy Sale Mar. 18th, heard me assert that Mrs. Rushford was the Editor of so & so. Immediately she asked, " Did you write

Salute to Malta? I read it over three or four times and thought of you straight away. I thought it was lovely." Was my face read [sic]. Why should I feel so embarrassed? Because of exposing my innermost thoughts to clumsy coarse prying fingers? They are not all like that surely. She wasn't. The quick-witted way she picked up the clue and added up the sum of her knowledge & found the correct answer, proves her to be of a fine intelligent character. Ah well. I've sent him three more, and a couple to John o' London. But I've no faith in the latter, just a great longing.

Then too, at the Feb. W.I. meeting I was given most points for my plain white scones. Not so many entries in the competition may be fortuitous, but still I was very pleased and to speak truly, the scones tasted good. I forgot all about them till after dinner. Luckily Mrs. Gill was baking and let me use her oven for ten minutes. Miss Hill gave an address on Happiness. She is an ex-Head Teacher, very small with great dignity, rather stiff, very deaf, harsh grating voice, nervous shaking hands, continually wiping her mouth with fine white hanky. She described different kinds of happiness, achievement, success, giving & receiving, wife's, mother's, etc. Remarked that of all happiness that of a mother on seeing her first baby must be the greatest. And a poor girl who had just given birth to a first baby dead born a few weeks ago, walked out in tears. Poor girl. But poor poor little old lady who wouldn't hurt anyone. The tears ran down her cheeks too, her lips refused to shape a word for some seconds and her hands couldn't keep still. But her head went up and by sheer will power she forced her voice to carry on and finish her talk. I felt so sorry for obviously she was desirous uplifting our hearts and here she had unwittingly opened the door to sorrow. When she had concluded and was drinking a cup of tea, The woman next to me said, "She brought it all back to me as well." And I found that poor soul, she had lost her first baby a year ago in a raid on Newcastle. Her father & mother in law had taken her little five month old son with them when she went into hospital to have a gathered breast attended to and on the very first night an earth mine had destroyed the whole street they lived in. The grandmother was found with the baby tight in her arms and the grandfather over both of them, all dead. She was not told for a fortnight. Dear God, the Sorrow and the Pain in the world. Is it not enough that life itself brings grief without himself making more?

I have received three letters from Will in the last two months, two of them only taking a week to reach me. It was good to see his writing again. It still looks the same, maybe a little firmer. He still finds little to say beyond that he is well, I must not worry and that he is longing for the Day when we are together again. They are all so alike. These thoughts must be always in his mind. Besides his letters are read, so he will not care to wax eloquent.

A letter from Joan tells me she is now living with Will's mother as Elsye has left her, but gives no reason for the flight. On Mar 14th Bill developed German Measles. He is not at all ill, full of life and has a great appetite. Eleanor as yet shows no signs of a spot but I have no doubt she will get plenty.

Malta is again being blitzed. Yesterday, Fri. night & Sat. morning 20 & 21st. brought 17 German planes down. Cheers. More reinforcements must be going to Libya. Ready for the Spring Offensive?

Sir Stafford Cripps arrived in India. Good luck go with him. Man of sense. Told story of man in his car who said of pedestrians in Moscow, "They walk across the streets as if they owned them."

Bring & Buy Sale Mon 18th. in Guild Hall in aid of H.G. man who lost his eyesight. Made over £60.

[Here ends her diary]

THREE LETTERS

I found these letters in Eleanor's box with the diaries. The first is written on lined paper from an exercise book in pencil and is clearly a draft which she kept. I was thrilled to bits to find it. Other than knowing I was born in 8 Elm Terrace, Mum had said little to me about my birth or I had forgotten anything she did say.

The other two are written on board SS Palestinian Prince, the liner on which she and Eleanor and I returned to England from Malta leaving Dad behind to face the coming siege of Malta for 4 long years. It is not clear whether the letters were posted (presumably when the ship docked in Southampton) to Dad or if so why he kept them. He doesn't seem to have kept any other of Mum's letters to him.

I

[A letter from my mother to my father,
who had been posted to Malta in March,
written from her bed in 8 Elm Terrace, Leadgate on Monday.]

12th October 1936

Darling PAPA,

Sounds good. Does it thrill you?

Your son and heir sends his greetings. It's a wonder you didn't hear him this morning when nurse washed him.

He arrived at 10 past four pm on Sat Oct 10th. So Dad's date was correct after all. He thinks he will set up a clinic for expectant mothers!

Fancy at 4 pm I only wanted to lie down and sleep for ever. At 4.15 I was champion. I began on Frid. morning but was not really bad till Sat. However, it's all over now – a most normal birth except for having to have a little fancy stitching by the doctor and even that was without chloroform. He said I was a big strong girl.

And now for our son. He was 8lbs weight and is ever so long. He has lots of fair hair – the colour yours is when you have no stuff on. That might come out but we all think he will be very fair as his eyebrows and lashes are. Frank says his lashes are like threads of gold.

He has such bright blue eyes. I hope they stay like that. And a most beautiful skin. Such pink cheeks and a little rosebud mouth.

Mother thinks he is very like you. I don't remember what you look like, sez me! The majority say he has your colouring and my features. What a mixture! My, how he is a devil to keep filled and that's like you. He nearly makes me cry every time he starts feeding as if he hasn't a mouthful before.

We would have written on Saturday but this Air Mail should get to you earlier. Besides we all waited from 4.10 till after six for the doctor and by the time everybody had visited us it was too late …

I've had a letter about my allowance today. 42/- arrears but it has to be paid back if your Birth Certificate is not found. Nurse says you have to write your Insurance Co. for a Maternity Benefit Form. Whoever you pay to I don't know.

Well darling names. How do you like JEREMY? (William of course will be one) David or Godfrey? Start thinking. I can't.

All we want is to see you darling and then we'll be in seventh Heaven.

All our love,
your wife and son.

II
[From Elsie to Will, Palestinian Prince][16]

20 July 1939

My very dear,

Here I am once again using a piece of paper not meant for you. It's the only piece left in the rack and I don't know who has used it.

Well the kids are fine today. We had a bit of a do with Billy at first. He wouldn't go out on deck because "the ship was moving." "Let's go home." Then later "Go back into the house." Today he's quite settled down. The Captain has been wonderful to him. Taken him round & played with him. Shown him his chameleons & Billy calls them lizards.

(The Ship is pitching fearfully.)

Eleanor of course has had to cut that double tooth, cut it Tuesday and was a little off colour. But this afternoon she has been her old self. Billy keeps asking where daddy is and Chan [Sgt Charles Chantry, Royal Signals]. I tell him at work and he is contented for a while. He trails the stewards round. Has found out how to work the Hoover and plagued the steward switching it on and off. He hangs round the pantry while I am at meals and eats as much again.

[In pencil] 21st Friday. I had to leave off yesterday. I felt quite groggy but a spot of brandy did me good.

[Back to ink] Yesterday was cold and windy. We all wore vests & jerseys. The kids are absolutely O.K. Eleanor was sitting on the Captain's knee playing with his brass buttons and trying to catch his pipe. They must have reminded her of you for when I said the buttons were like Daddy's she looked round for you. Someone else mentioned Daddy to her and she looked at the door to see you clapping her hands. Her face dropped when you didn't come.

They are ever so good really. Tonight I bathed them at 5, dinner 5.30. They were asleep at 6.15. Tea at 7am

Meals:	Kids	Me
Breakfast	8 am	8.30
Lunch	12	12.30
Tea	4	
Dinner	5.30pm	6pm
Supper	9pm	

And the food is very good. Only the hors d'oeuvres are not so good as the Bay boats. But I do enjoy being waited on as you know to your sorrow.

We have passed Gib. Tonight at 6pm. What a grand sight. I wondered if I might ever live there. It would be queer if you were stationed there, but not for a few years. The sea has been very calm today. I wish you were here to stargaze with me tonight. I feel quite romantic but it's a waste of time. The Third Officer, a handsome, dark, young man sits at my table but he hasn't fallen for my charms. The other passengers are very decent, very sociable.

I keep wondering what you are doing and how you are. Take care of yourself dearest. If anything were to happen I should regret leaving you all my life. You are so necessary and precious to us.

III
From Elsie to Will Palestinian Prince

26th July 1939

My darling,

After an interval I resume your letter. No, we've not had trouble. But I have only had the opportunity to write at night as you can guess. And I have been so tired. I have been in bed by 8.30. These little – have been awake any time between 4.30 and 5.30 am. Yes they have had & sleep during the day also but even I have slept one or two days. I shall be glad tomorrow when we land.

Have you been worrying about our arrival? Did you expect my cable yesterday? We will not dock till 5-ish pm. But there is a good express to NC [Newcastle] at 6 pm. I am sorry to have to travel so late with the kids but they will have to go through with it. I only hope Ella is there.

We have not had a bad trip, although 3 ladies were down for two or three days. I have been my usual self. Bill never felt a thing. Eleanor was sick on Saturday night but I blame some kidney soup. She was O.K. on Sunday. They are both at home now. The Captain has Eleanor on his knee at meal times and the First Officer takes Bill up on the bridge. They have their meals in our cabin but they follow me into the dining room. Bill plays at being steward ('ceward' he says) with a menu and now Eleanor stands with them by the sideboard.

They both look a lot fatter and have a nice fresh colour.

And after all that, how are you? I have you always in my mind wondering what you are doing, how you are. I do hope the heat is not too much for you. You should benefit by that afternoon sleep or are you having to work?

Later.

I had to stop to listen to '8 Bells' Were you listening to it? It was grand.

Did you get all finished up at the Ravelin?[17] I bet you had a job. You would be glad to see the last of us. But oh dear I do wish I had you near again. I could eat you tonight. I can't go to sleep without you near. So hurry up. Threaten the Major with any old thing if he doesn't let you come to me. Billy was waving to Daddy out of the porthole today and Eleanor stood to shout too. He says "God bless Daddy and send him home soon."

I must close now darling. Take care of yourself for our sake. I love you so.

Yours,

Elsie. XX

Showing snaps today. What a good looking man your hubby is. He's marvellous. He's mine, says I.

XXXXX

APPENDICES

APPENDICES

APPENDIX I

Dramatis Personae

Grandma Jewitt, a widow nee Isabella Maudlin. She was born in Annfield Plain in 1869. She died in August 1947.

Her husband, my grandfather **George Jewitt**, was born in Leadgate on 9th May 1869 and died on 6th August 1938 while we were in Malta. This was hard for Mum who was very fond of her father.

Elsie, my Mum, was born 13th April 1906 in Leadgate. She was bright and went for teacher training in Yorkshire where she met my Dad. They were married on Boxing Day 1934 at St Ives Church in Leadgate. Dad, a Lance Corporal, was posted to Malta on 3rd March 1936. I was born on 10th October that year at Leadgate and Mum and I joined Dad in Malta later. Eleanor was born on 26th May 1938 in the Military Families Hospital, Imtarfa Malta.

Ella Jewitt, Mum's younger sister was born in Leadgate on 16th April 1909. In 1941 she was single and 'going out' with

Frank Loughran, for some 10 years. They didn't get married till after Grandma died. He was a Roman Catholic and I believe both parents were against them marrying. In 1941 she went to work on munitions in Bolton, doing well and becoming a civil servant. **Snip** was our dog, a lovely Fox Terrier.

Eve Nolloth, Mum's elder sister born in Leadgate on 9th January 1904. She was married to **Ralph Nolloth** who worked in Consett Iron & Steel Works. Their son, **John**, was a couple of years older than me and an only child and spoiled in Mum's eyes. They lived in Delves Lane on the other side of Consett. They had a dog called Judy.

George, Mum's only brother who left Leadgate and his family to go and work in Dunchurch near Rugby. He married **Queen** (Frances Ada Sawford) in April 1939 and they had 2 sons, **Colin** and **Paul** who were born in 1942 and 1945 respectively.

Aunty Nellie Carrick nee Jewitt (born in Leadgate in the winter of 1881) was my grandfather's sister and lived in Scotswood outside Newcastle. Her daughter(?) was Lily.

Uncle Joe Jewitt (born in Leadgate on 19th January 1876) was my grandfather's brother, Joseph, who was unmarried and lived sometime in Jarrow.

My Dad, **William Leslie Harry Crouch**, was born in Boscombe Bournemouth on 29th August 1910. His mother, my Gran, was **Dora Gates** and she was born on 29th September 1888 and died 21st October 1968. She lived in Branksome Bournemouth at 33 Yarmouth Road. My Grandfather, **William Thomas Crouch**, was a cabinet maker, then a chauffeur (domestic coachman) at Great Chalfield in Boscombe. He married **Dora** in Bournemouth on 18th December, 1909. He died on 21st December 1923 from TB at the age of 38. It is sad that I never knew either grandfather.

Dad's brothers were **Ronald Ernest Crouch** and **Cyril Wilson Crouch**. Ron was born 16th May 1916. He joined the

Royal Artillery and was killed just after D Day in Normandy on 11th July 1944 and is buried in the St Manvieu War Cemetery, Cheux. I never knew him and it was only later I got to know his daughter, **Gaye Crouch** born on 24th February 1940. Ron married **Elsye Lillian Allen** in 1938 and while he was away in the army Elsye lived with Gran until for reasons unknown they parted as is recorded in the 1942 diary. She died in 1994 in Parkstone, Poole.

Cyril was dad's younger brother. He was born in Boscombe near Bournemouth on 6th June 1912. He married **Joan Lane** who was born on 28th October 1915. He joined the RAF. They had 2 children, **Michael** born in 1943 and **Nicholas** born in 1948. Joan moved in to live with Gran after Elsye moved out.

Nellie Loughran was Frank's sister.

The Crosby's. They lived across the way from us in Leadgate – our front room window looked onto the front of their house. They were considered somewhat up market since their house wasn't a council house and moreover had a bay window upstairs and downstairs. **Freddie Crosby** (Freddie lad as my mother called him but not to his face) owned a wool shop on Front Street. He had one leg shorter than the other and wore a built-up boot. **Edna**, his wife, was a pleasant woman whom my mother obviously thought was much put upon by Freddie. There were two children, **Margaret** who was older than me and **David** whose birth is recorded in the diary. I last heard of Margaret as having retired as a school head and living in Lanchester.

The Laxes. Old **Mrs. Lax** lived with her family up from the Crosbys. There was **Harvey**, **John** and **Hannah**. They were great friends of Grandma's and in and out of our house. Ella years later spent a great deal of time looking after Mrs. Lax when she was failing.

The **Browns** lived on the other side of the Crosby's -another house with a bay window. Alistair was Mr. Brown's son and about my age or perhaps younger.

The Gills. Next door neighbours. **Mrs. Gill**, a widow with 3 sons and a daughter. **Ivor**, the oldest, **Derrick**, **Margie** and **Mervyn** the youngest. Mervyn's birthday was the same as mine and he was 6 years older than me. She was always in our house although I can't remember going in their house. The two older boys were keen on motor bikes. The family was very staunchly Salvation Army and the boys played in Leadgate SA Band. The noise of them practising trumpet, trombone and euphonium is a lasting memory.

The Seymours. Mum knew **Ethel Walker** before she became Mrs. Seymour. Her children were special friends of Eleanor's and they played together in their (comparatively) large house off Front street. **Margaret** was the elder and **Helen** the closer in age to Eleanor.

Mrs. Hall and her daughter **Marion** lived opposite in Ash Terrace. **Mrs. Green** lived down Elm Terrace as did **Mrs. Coulson**.

My friends were **Barry Bell** later to become a policeman in Leadgate, **Alan Agar** whose father was in the navy, **Gerry Macdonald** a Roman Catholic and therefore a curiosity to me and **Clifford Pears** whose father, we believed, used his belt frequently on his unfortunate children.

I remember very well that momentous day in October when I started school. **Miss Hall** was the Head and was a large lady and very nice. **Miss Love** the infants, or babies, teacher was lovely and her classroom the nicest of them all. It had a huge fireplace and a blazing fire which was kept burning through the cold weather.

She was a marvellous story teller and kept me enthralled with her readings.

Eve and **Annie Ross** had a small haberdashery to which I used to be sent with an order from my mother written on a tightly folded piece of paper. I was given in exchange a brown paper parcel. Nobody mentioned what the parcel contained.

Boustead's was the shop on the corner of Durham Road and Front Street. It sold everything except groceries. Mum's main purchase there were cigarettes or cigs as she called them. They came in tens, twenties or just fives. The lowest of the low were Woodbines which she hated and only bought as a last resort. She would chase round the shops in Leadgate buying up cigarettes wherever she found some. It's ironic that she was to die from lung cancer in 1969. **Walter Wilson's** was the grocery store on Front Street where Mum bought her rations. **The Post Office** was where Mum drew her allowance and sent cables to my father in Malta.

Vera the milk girl I don't really remember but I do remember our milk being delivered by a horse drawn milk float from Herdman's farm at Redwell Hills. The milk was measured out in a copper ladle from huge churns into our jug. We kept the jug in the pantry on the window shelf which faced north. The milk was protected from the flies by a gauze cloth weighed down with coloured beads sewn in the edge.

APPENDIX II

Family Photographs

Ralph Nolloth and George Jewitt ca. 1930.

*Dad and Mum
after their wedding in December 1934.*

Dad with Eleanor in Malta ca. 1938.

Mum with Eleanor and Bill in Malta ca. 1939.

Dad with Eleanor and Bill in Malta ca. 1939.

Eleanor and Bill in Valetta ca. 1939.

Mum, Eleanor and Bill in studio photo ca. 1940.

*Mum in the front garden
in the snow ca. 1941.*

*Eleanor and Bill in the front garden at 8 Elm
Terrace by the Anderson air raid shelter ca 1941.*

Mum with Eleanor and Bill outside back door, 8 Elm Terrace, ca. 1941.

Dad in Malta.

Dad in Malta ca. 1941.

Dad in Malta.

Dad ca. 1944.   *Ella ca. 1942.*

Mum, Eleanor and Bill ca. 1943.   *Mum and Dad ca. 1944.*

*Granma Jewitt in Liverpool with
Cedric, born in Liverpool, 1948.*

Gran Crouch ca. 1950.

*Grandad Jewitt at back door,
8 Elm Terrace, date unknown.*

*Frank Loughran and Ella Jewitt
at their wedding ca. August 1952.*

APPENDIX III

The Places Mentioned in the Diary

Hat and Feather was a pub on the top of a bleak windswept hill to the north of Leadgate on the old Watling Street. It was frequently blocked by snow in the winter.

Delves Lane was a village to the south of Consett and was where Eve lived.

The Dene was a lovely wooded valley south of Redwell Hill's Farm where we often walked. It was a favourite place for Sunday school picnics in summer. I remember the steep grassy slopes dotted with golden prickly broom. Skylarks burbled above in blue skies and the air was heavy with scent of wild flowers. I remember too rolling Easter Eggs down the side of the Dene. Paste Eggs they were called; hard boiled eggs whose shells were stained with dyes a green or blue or red or a streaky mix of them all.

APPENDIX IV

Books Referred to by Mum in Order of Appearance in her Diary

'Oriental Assembly', TE Lawrence

'Forbidden Road', Rosita Forbes

'Ben Sees it Through', J Jefferson Farjeon

'By the Waters of Babylon', Robert Neumann

'English Ways', Jack Hilton

'No Hearts to Break', Susan Ertz

'American Wife', Brother Jerome

'Journal of Katherine Mansfield'

'Testament of Friendship', Vera Brittain

'Nanking Road', Vicki Baum

'South Riding', Winifred Holtby

'The World As I See It', Albert Einstein

'Dear Octopus', Dodie Smith

'The Lights Go Down', Erika Mann

'The Polish Gold', RM Low & Robert Westerby

'Lover's Meeting', Lady Eleanor Smith

'Quest for Sheba: In the Footsteps of the Arabian Queen', Norman Stone Pearn, Vincent Barlo

'The Light of Heat', Emlyn Williams

'The West Wind of Love', Compton Mackenzie

'South to Samarkand', Ethel Mannin

'An Epic of the Gestapo: the Story of a Strange Search', Paul Dukes

'Right Ho Jeeves', PG Wodehouse

'Sleepers East', Fred Nebel

'Mein Kampf', Adolph Hitler

'Hitler Speaks: A Series of Political Conversations With Adolf Hitler', Hermann Rauschning

'Night Rider', Robert Penn Norren

'Fanny by Gaslight', Michael Sadleir

'The Valley of the Assassins', Freya Stark

'TE Lawrence by his friends', ed. AW Lawrence

'Self Portrait: A Novel of His Own Life', Gilbert Frankau

'Revolt in the Desert', TE Lawrence

'Seven Pillars of Wisdom', TE Lawrence

'Memory Hold-the-Door', John Buchan

'John Brown Autobiography (S Shields boy makes Good)'

'War by Revolution', Francis Williams

'Dare to Live', Ida Hurst

'Testament of Joad', CM Joad

'My Country and My People', Lin Yutang

'New Order', CP Purdam

'The Astonishing Island', Winifred Holtby

'Freedom in the Modern World', John MacMurray

'This is our World', Kurt Lubinski

'Faked Passports', Dennis Wheatley

'The Story of San Michele', Axel Munthe

'Letters of TE Lawrence'

'Thus Germany Spoke – Collection of Scraps'

'The Glorious Adventure', Richard Halliburton

'Women and Children Last', Beverley Nichols

'The Road to Nowhere', Maurice Walsh

'Words Win Wars – Propaganda, the Mightiest Weapon of All', John Hargrave

'Savoy! Corsica! Tunis!', Bernard Newman

'Chaffinch's', HW Freeman

'Not I, But the Wind', Frieda Lawrence (TEL's wife)

'The Flying Visit', Peter Fleming

'Scoop', Evelyn Waugh

'Augustus John Drawings', Lillian Browse (Ed.)

'Our Fellow Men', HV Morton

'Fire Over England', AEW Mason

'Brave New World', Aldous Huxley

'The Holy Terror', HG Wells

'In His Master's Footsteps', HV Morton

APPENDIX V

Housekeeping

In another old notebook now lacking a cover, Mum has made the following shopping lists. The year is not clear. It is written in pencil, but not so difficult to read. The first entry is dated Aug. 24th 1942. All the prices are, of course, in Pounds, Shillings and Pence (L.s.d.) She also wrote the notes for a talk on Malta she was to give to the WI on 2nd March 1943.

Housekeeping Jan 16th [crossed out] – 22nd

		£ - s - d
Mon 19th	Milk 7½d, Bread 4½d, Cabbage, Sugar 1 - 0½, tobacco 3 - 8	7 - 0
Tue 20th	Milk 7½, Bread 4½, Potatoes 10, sausage	3 - 2
Wed 21st	Rations Ev milk B Beans Egg Domestos	10 - 8
	Sheep's head 1/- Milk 7½, Bread 4½	2 - 0
	Sprouts 7d, Oranges 1/4, Parsley 7	2 - 0
	Fish 1/9, Tea 11	2 - 8
Thur 22nd	Milk 7½,Bread 4½, Colgate 1/4	2 - 4
Fri 23rd	Tea, Sugar, C Flakes, 2 Jams, Gelatine, Biscuits	12 - 8½
	Fish, Pork	6 - 10
	Cabbage, Celery	1 - 6
	Milk, Bread, Cake, Buns	2 - 5½
	Papers 7/10, Writing Paper 2/9, 10 Cigs 1/8	12 - 3
Sat 24th	Milk 1/8, Bread 9d, Pie 2/6, Cake 1/9	6 - 8
	Oranges 1/4, Onions 7d, Apples 1/-	2 - 11
		£3 - 16 -10
	Insurance 1/3 Windows 1/3	
Mon 26th	Milk, Bread	1 - 0½
Tue 27th	Milk, Bread	1 - 0½
	Fish 1/-, Oranges 1/4, Sprouts 1/2,	3 - 6

	Butter, Marg, Lard, Bacon, Tin, Mussels, Crab Paste	7 - 8
	Biscuits, Sugar, Dates, G Paper, Syrup	3 - 10½
	Logs	11 - 9
Wed 28th	Milk, Bread, Pastilles	2 - 6½
	Cigs, Tobacco	7 -1½
Thur 29th	Milk, Bread	1 - 5
	Onions, Apples	1 - 11
	Mujol[?], Face Cloth, Magnesia, Su[?]	8 - 6
	Stewing meat	1 - 3
	Firelighters	1 - 4
	Shoes - heeled	2 - 0
Fri 30th	Milk, Bread	1 - 0
	Sausages	1 - 4
	Meat	5 - 6
	Milk 1/8, Bread 9, Cake	4 - 5
	Carrots, Sprouts, Shoe Polish	2 - 0
	Fish & Chips	3 - 9
	Ev milk, Biscuits, Dr[ied] Egg,Flour, Prunes, Marm[alade], S Powder	8 - 10
		82 - 11½
	Papers 4/-, Sweets 1/7, Flannel, Cotton, Elastic	5 - 7
		94 - 1½

[Don't ask about the Arithmetic!]

July 8th	Insurance 1 - 3/1 - 0/6d/1 - 4/	4 - 1
	Agent	3 - 0
	School Dinners	4 - 2
	Savings	5 - 0
	Papers	4 - 0

Aug 24th 1942

	Players (Cigarettes) 20	2(s) - 0(d)
	3pts (Ration points) 3 pkts Maltesers	7½
	2 pts ¼ Sharps Toffees	6
	Graingers [Dept Store in Newcastle]	6 - 6
	2 S(avings) Certificates	30 - 0
	Mum [Granma Jewitt]	20 - 0

Nov 26th	Groceries	15 - 6
	Books	4

Nov 27th	Meat	4 - 8
	Green Groceries	1 - 7
	Sweets	1 - 0
	Garage (Battery charging?)	1 - 3
	[Gas] Mantles	2 - 3

No date	Rations etc. groceries	30 - 0
	Meat	8 - 0
	Milk	9 - 3½
	Bread	7 - 0
	Vegetables, fruit	7 - 0
	Diners	5 - 10
	Buses	2 - 6

Finally, although not exactly coming under the heading of 'Housekeeping', the following notes on a 'Talk on Malta' are included in the same pages.

Talk on Malta
March 2nd '43, Grove W. Institute. Consett.

1. Intro
Importance of Malta. Position. Size, Climate, Rocky ground & coastline. Sands.

2. Valletta
Harbour, Barracca Wall, Bastions, Buildings, Streets, goats, Gharrozzi. Churches (Bells) "Bells, smells, yells"

3. Country Outside
Fields, water mills and mules, Clover wheat beans cabbages etc. Carts. Hilly roads, sea, dry stone walling, Patchwork fields. Villages. Houses (shut up look). Jalousies, high walls, half doors.

4. Gardens
Peanut man. Frank who did baskets and sachels [sic]. Flowers. Irrigation. San Antonio (green) Spring Melita Road.

5. The Maltese
Looks, gentle. Courteous. Generous. Warm hearted. Love of children. Good business people. Bargaining probably now stopped.

Living. Use of oil (for cooking) . no baking bread. Lacework, embroidery, weaving, dress making. Poor but very cheerful & happy. Beggars. Orphans.

6. Festas
Church processions, Every Friday in lent, Holy Thursday. Good Friday. St Paul. The Virgin Mary.

7. Conclusion.

ENDNOTES

1. *See entry for 5th February 1941.*
    JB Priestley, author, playwright and broadcaster, broadcast regularly from 1940 and through 1941 on the radio on a Sunday evening. The 'Postscript' was very popular and drew peak audiences of 16 million. Only Churchill was more popular with the listeners.

2. *See entry for 1st March 1941.*
    We had no mains electricity in 8 Elm Terrace in those days, only gas for lighting and cooking, paid for by a gas meter which took old pennies. The radio, or wireless as it was more commonly known, was powered by a battery. We had a rechargeable accumulator. This was a heavy glass 'bottle' with a carrying handle and contained an acid (sulphuric, I think) and electrodes. It had to be charged up regularly at the village garage.

3. *See entry for 26th March 1941.*
    Ann Driver's 'Music and Movement' programmes were broadcast by the BBC and were very popular among parents and children.

4. *See entry for 27th March 1941.*

    King Peter II came to the Yugoslav throne aged eleven after
    his father was assassinated in 1934. His father's cousin, Prince
    Paul, headed the Regency. Paul declared Yugoslavia would join
    with Hitler on 25th March 1941 and two days later Peter was
    proclaimed King and ousted Prince Paul in a bloodless coup.
    He declared against the Germans. The German army attacked
    Yugoslavia and Greece simultaneously and on 17th April the
    Yugoslav government was forced to surrender. The King and his
    government fled to England.

5. *See entry for 14th May 1941.*

    On the 10th May 1941 Hitler's deputy disappeared from Germany
    during a test flight. A similar plane later landed in Scotland that
    same night. A man later claiming to be Rudolf Hess was found
    in the area and arrested. This man asserted that he had come to
    broker a peace with Britain. He was taken to the Tower of London
    and, after the war ended, he was tried with other senior Nazis
    in the Nuremberg Trials. He was subsequently sentenced to life
    imprisonment in Berlin's Spandau jail.

    There is speculation that Hess was murdered by British
    Intelligence services, although two autopsies could not confirm
    this. Some claim that the prisoner tried at Nuremberg was a
    double willingly impersonating Hess. The truth, it seems, will
    never be known.

6. *See entry for 21st June 1941.*

    Operation Barbarossa, as the invasion of Russia was codenamed,
    had been planned by the German High Command since October
    1940. Now with England on the back foot, Hitler felt that the
    time was ripe to attack Russia. The invasion of Yugoslavia had
    only delayed his plans. He was misled about Russian strengths
    and capabilities after their poor showing against the Finns. Hitler
    invaded Russia on 21st June 1941 and Russia became our Ally
    against Nazism.

7. *See entry for 27th June 1941.*

    'Knute Rockne, All American' was the title of a film released in 1940 starring Pat O'Brien and Ronald Reagan. It told the biographical story of Knute Rockne, the famous Notre Dame American football coach.

8. *See entry for 21st July 1941.*

    Pelaw is a district that forms part of the Metropolitan Borough of Gateshead in Tyne and Wear, in north-east England. Originally just a small railway junction, when the Co-operative organisation was expanding into the North-East it was chosen as a central, well-connected place in which to build their factories. CWS stands for the Co-operative Wholesale Society, which was the manufacturing division of the then burgeoning Co-op company. A huge and diverse number of products were made by these factories throughout the Twentieth century.

9. *See entry for 14th August 1941.*

    Clement Attlee was the leader of the Labour party from 1935–55, and held various posts in the coalition government which was in office during the Second World War, including Lord Privy Seal from 1940–42. He was Deputy Prime Minister in Churchill's absences abroad and succeeded him as Prime Minister when Labour won the 1945 election at the end of the war.

10. *See entry for 14th August 1941.*

    In August 1941 Roosevelt met Churchill on the battleship HMS Prince of Wales off Newfoundland. They proclaimed the so-called 'Atlantic Charter' which set out the postwar aims agreed between the United States and Britain. The main aims were: peace and security, freedom of government and free economy.

11. *See entry for 4th September 1941.*

    AFS men were members of the Auxiliary Fire Service which was formed in 1938 and was mobilised on the 1st of September 1939 and disbanded at the end of the Second World War.

12. *See entry for 27th September 1941.*

   Jacqueline Dalya was an American stage and screen actress.

13. *See entry for 14th and 15th November 1941.*

   HMS Ark Royal, an aircraft carrier, was the fourth ship of the Royal Navy to bear that name. It was part of Operation Perpetual carrying Swordfish aircraft to Malta when it was torpedoed on 13th November 1941 in the Western Mediterranean by German Submarine U-81. It sank the next day with the loss of only one life.

14. *See Memo, 10th December 1941.*

   The Japanese Imperial Navy made a surprise attack on the US Pacific fleet at anchor in Pearl Harbour, Hawaii, on the morning of 7th December, 1941. The Japanese aim was to prevent American interference in their plans to attack South East Asia and the Britain. The attack was a great shock to the American people and along with Germany's declaration of war against America, made the way clear for President Roosevelt to enter the war on Britain's side.

15. *See entry for 1st January*

   'With Allenby in Palestine and Lawrence in Arabia' was a film directed by Lowell Thomas in 1919. It featured original footage of the Middle East campaign with TE Lawrence and Edmund Allenby. In 1924 Thomas wrote 'With Lawrence in Arabia'. It is not clear whether Mum is referring to the film or the book. She clearly got Thomas' name wrong. I cannot find who Todd Colney was.

16. *See 2nd letter, 20th July 1939.*

   SS Palestinian Prince belonged to the Prince & Rio Cape Line and was built in 1936. Its funnel was black with a thin red band above a thicker red band containing the feathers of the Prince of Wales. It was 1,965 tons. It served until 1960.

17. *See 3rd letter, 26th July 1939.*

   Ravelin was a fortified area in a defensive wall with enfilading fire and so on. It was the name of the part of Valletta which housed troops and was bombed by the Germans.